Saint Wilfrid

John Nankivell

Published in Great Britain in 2002
Society for Promoting Christian Knowledge
Holy Trinity Church
Marylebone Road
London NW1 4DU

British Library Cataloguing-in-Publication Data

A catalogue record for this book is available from the British Library

ISBN 0-281-05445-2

Typeset by Trinity Typing, Wark-on-Tweed
Printed in Great Britain by Bookmarque Ltd, Croydon, Surrey

Contents

❧❧

Battles and the Succession to the Northumbrian Throne

Date	Place	Significance of the Battle
603	Degsastan (place no longer known)	Ethelfrid defeated the Scots
614	Chester	Ethelfrid defeated the British
616	River Idle	Edwin defeated Ethelfrid and succeeded
633	Hatfield Chase	A British-Mercian alliance defeated Edwin
634	Heavenfield, near Hexham	Oswald defeated the British-Mercian alliance and succeeded
642	Oswestry (Maserfelth)	The British defeated the Northumbrians; Oswald was killed and Oswy succeeded
655	Winwaed, near Leeds	Oswy defeated Penda of Mercia
685	Dunnichen Moss, near Forfar	The Picts defeated Egfrid

Eanfled's Family Tree

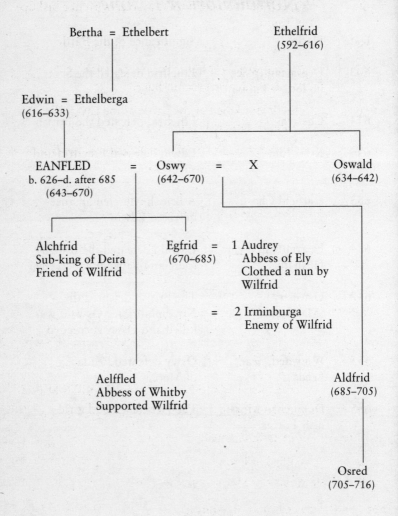

Dates in brackets are dates of rule in Northumbria.

Time Chart

560	Queen Bertha, the Frank, arrives with her bishop in Kent.
584	Edwin is exiled to Ynys Mon (Anglesey).
597	Columba dies on Iona. Augustine reaches Canterbury.
616	Ethelfrid is killed at the battle at the River Idle. Eanfled's father, Edwin, succeeds.
625	Ethelberga comes to Northumbria with her bishop Paulinus and marries Edwin.
626	Eanfled is born on Easter night.
627	Edwin is baptized by Bishop Paulinus.
633	Edwin is killed at Hatfield Chase. Ethelberga returns to Kent with her daughter.
634	Oswald and Aidan found Lindisfarne. Birth of Wilfrid.
642	Oswald killed at Oswestry, Oswy succeeds.
643	Eanfled returns to Northumbria and marries Oswy.
648	Eanfled directs Wilfrid to Lindisfarne.
652	Eanfled sends Wilfrid to her cousin, the King of Kent.
653	Wilfrid meets Benedict Biscop and travels to Lyon.
655	Wilfrid in Rome.
656–659	Wilfrid in Lyon.
660	Wilfrid is Abbot of Ripon.
664	The synod of Whitby. Wilfrid is chosen as bishop.

665	Wilfrid is consecrated bishop in Gaul.
666–668	Wilfrid is a peripatetic bishop in Mercia and Kent. Chad is Bishop of York.
668–690	Theodore is Archbishop of Canterbury.
669–678	Wilfrid is Bishop of York. Ripon and Hexham churches are built. Biscop founds his monastery at Wearmouth.
678–679	Wilfrid brings the gospel to the pagan Frisians.
679	Wilfrid appeals to the Roman synod.
680	King Egrid throws Wilfrid into gaol. Hilda of Whitby dies. Bede enters the monastery at Wearmouth.
681–686	Wilfrid is a missionary in Sussex.
685	King Egfrid is killed by the Picts in the battle of Dunnichen Moss.
686	Theodore and Wilfrid are reconciled.
687	Wilfrid is Abbot of Lindisfarne.
688–692	Wilfrid is back in York.
692–703	Wilfrid is in Mercia. Wilfrid's monk Willibrord goes to Frisia as bishop. Lindisfarne Gospels are written.
702	The council of Austerfield.
703–704	Wilfrid's second appeal to Rome.
706	The council of Nidd.
709	Wilfrid's last instructions and death.

Queen Eanfled's Britain

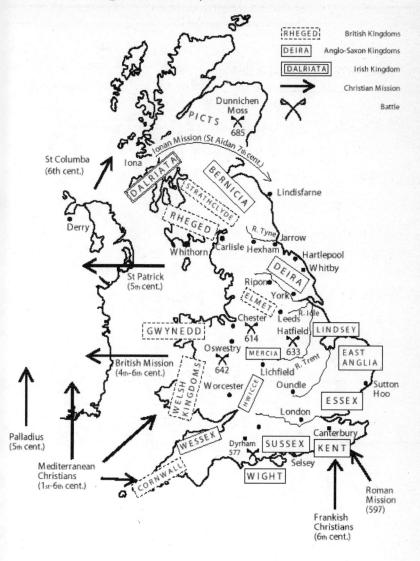

RHEGED — British Kingdoms
DEIRA — Anglo-Saxon Kingdoms
DALRIATA — Irish Kingdom
→ Christian Mission
✗ Battle

PICTS

Dunnichen Moss
685

Iona
St Columba (6th cent.)

Ionan Mission (St Aidan 7th cent.)

DALRIATA

BERNICIA

STRATHCLYDE

RHEGED

Derry

Whithorn   Carlisle   Hexham

Lindisfarne

R. Tyne   Jarrow

Hartlepool
Whitby

St Patrick (5th cent.)

DEIRA

Ripon
York

ELMET

R. Idle

GWYNEDD

Chester
614

Leeds

Hatfield
633

LINDSEY

British Mission (4th–6th cent.)

Oswestry

MERCIA

EAST ANGLIA

WELSH KINGDOMS

642

Lichfield

R. Trent

Palladius (5th cent.)

Worcester

HWICCE

Oundle

ESSEX

Sutton Hoo

London

Mediterranean Christians (1st–6th cent.)

WESSEX

CORNWALL

Dyrham
577

SUSSEX

Canterbury

KENT

Selsey

WIGHT

Roman Mission (597)

Frankish Christians (6th cent.)

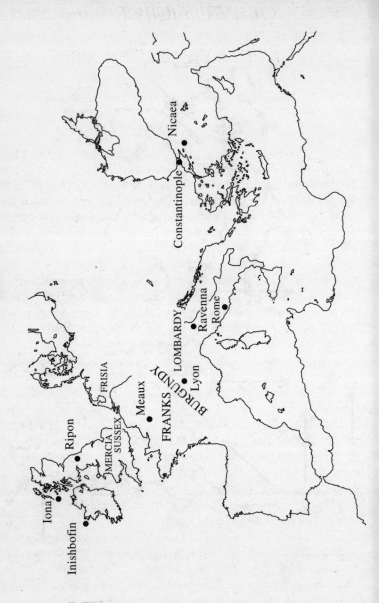

Europe

Iona
Inishbofin
Ripon
MERCIA
SUSSEX
FRISIA
Meaux
FRANKS
BURGUNDY
LOMBARDY
Lyon
Ravenna
Rome
Constantinople
Nicaea

Introduction

St Wilfrid and his Biographer

Wilfrid was born in 634 and was buried 75 years later in his native Northumbria. He had a great and lasting influence in the north of England, but for many years he was an exile in other parts of Britain and on the continent. Wherever he went he made an impact, as he was a man of unshakeable conviction, enormous energy and considerable powers of persuasion. His life was told soon after his death by a monk of his own monastery of Ripon, the priest Stephen, often known as Eddius.

Whenever a story is told, the unusual is given more attention than the everyday. Striking and dramatic events seem worth recording; not those things that are familiar to everyone. Warfare leaves more records than peacetime. Family albums are full of holiday snaps, but rarely record the washing-up.

So it is with Eddius' life of Wilfrid. Eddius wrote for the monks of Ripon and Hexham and, as they were familiar with the daily life of the monastery, he makes no mention of it. We hear about the shipwreck on the south coast, when Wilfrid was set upon by the wild South Saxons, but learn nothing about the daily life of his monastery in Sussex. Eddius and his fellow monks were steeped in worship, so this is not described. They were familiar with the running of the Church, so the proceedings of regular church councils are not recorded. But we do read about the unusual meeting at Whitby and the shenanigans at the synod of Austerfield, where Wilfrid was put in the dock.

Wilfrid was a counsellor and confidant of kings, a missionary to the South Saxons and the pagans of Frisia, and a bishop in many kingdoms. But first of all he was a monk. At the age of 14 he entered the monastery at Lindisfarne. Sixty-one years later he died at Oundle, in one of the many monasteries that he had founded. Wherever he was, at home or abroad, travelling or in prison, he prayed and sang the psalms as he would have done in his own monastery. To understand him, we need an insight into the monastic life, its daily rhythms, its architecture, iconography and music, its patterns of work and worship.

Wilfrid lived in a world of repeated warfare between the newly established Germanic kingdoms of Britain. The Church had the task of preaching the gospel to the pagans and establishing the institutions to sustain the Christian life of the newly converted. At the same time, it had to cope with the variations in custom and practice between its British, Irish and Anglo-Saxon adherents, which could become points of conflict, sometimes sharpened by experience of inter-ethnic warfare.

Kings, whatever their motivation, were deeply interested in the Church, and bishops were inevitably affected by political changes. As these were often violent, it is not surprising that the lives of those involved in leadership were touched by controversy. Wilfrid was among those who found themselves in conflict with kings and archbishops. But most of his many years were peaceful, and his work in Northumbria, Mercia and Sussex had an influence that has lasted to our own days. This book tells the tale of Wilfrid's life against the backdrop of the ever-changing political world of the seventh century.

Contrasts are sometimes drawn between Wilfrid and the Irish saints. Wilfrid has been portrayed as a disputatious bishop interested in power and wealth, in contrast to the other-worldly mildness of the 'Celtic' saints and those, like Cuthbert, who stand in that tradition. There are differences that follow from the particular work and life of each, but the Christian faith that unites them is far more significant than the contrasts between them. The final part of the book discusses some of the controversies in which Wilfrid was involved, and the views of him held by those of various ideological stripes.

Part I

Queen Eanfled's Britain

Prologue

Young Man at Court

In 648 the 14-year-old Wilfrid appeared before the Northumbrian queen, Eanfled, asking for her advice and protection. His handsome bearing and sharp intellect made an immediate impact on her and she responded without hesitation to his request. He wished, he said, to 'give himself to the service of God'.

In such few words are we introduced to Wilfrid and to the most important encounter of his life. Queen Eanfled opened the way for him to spend the next 12 years in the great centres of western Christendom – Lindisfarne, Canterbury, Lyon and Rome. As his mentor and protector, she guided him through the first days of his adulthood. When he returned to Northumbria at the age of 26 he was fully formed, intellectually and spiritually mature, eager and well equipped to embark on his life's work.

Eanfled's husband and sons were to determine the political landscape of Wilfrid's adult world; her daughter and sister-in-law were to make crucial interventions during his darkest moments. Eanfled was of mixed descent: Deiran, Kentish and Frankish. The names Deira and Kent are Celtic, but Eanfled's Deiran forebears were the Angles who had settled in northern Britain and her Kentish family was of Jutish origin. The offspring of three Germanic peoples, she found herself queen of a realm that included Britons, Irish and Picts. It was in the complex world of Eanfled's Britain that Wilfrid was destined to struggle 'in the service of God'.

1

The Peoples of Britain and Ireland

Wilfrid was an Angle, born in Northumbria. By the time he was born, many of his people had been converted to Christianity, and he was brought up in a Christian home. At the heart of the Christianity of his homeland was the Irish monastery of Lindisfarne and it was here that Wilfrid spent his teenage years. He then spent a formative time in Lyon and Rome, before returning to Northumbria where he became bishop.

Most of his life was spent in his native Northumbria and in the neighbouring kingdom of Mercia, in central Britain. But he was to find himself exiled to other kingdoms. And twice he made the journey to Rome to appeal to the Pope against decisions made by the Archbishop of Canterbury.

Many of Wilfrid's fellow Anglo-Saxons remained pagan and much of his work was devoted to bringing them to Christ and teaching and supporting them in their new faith. He spent five years as a missionary to the pagan Saxons of Sussex, during which time the Church became firmly established there. He was also the first to preach the gospel to the people of Frisia, and the conversion of the Frisians was completed by one of his Northumbrian monks. He was, therefore, the first of the Anglo-Saxon missionaries to the continent. In the eighth century, others such as Boniface of Crediton were to continue this work and carry the faith to the Germanic peoples of the continent.

But Wilfrid worked not only with Anglo-Saxons, but also with the British, the Irish and the Picts. Before embarking on his story, let us have a look at the background of each of these four peoples of seventh-century Britain.

When the Romans arrived, the British were the only people between the south coast and what is now the Scottish border. North of them were the Picts and some settlers from Ireland. The ancient Atlantic seaways connected the British to their Celtic cousins in Ireland and Gaul, and to the wider world of Spain, North Africa and the rest of the Mediterranean. The earliest Christians probably arrived by these sea routes, as did the monastic traditions of Egypt and Palestine. The Romans brought new institutions and patterns of life. Their roads and cities changed things dramatically, but they often incorporated indigenous traditions and structures. Local government was organized according to the old tribal boundaries, and the Celtic gods were given hospitality in the Roman pantheon. The shrine of Aqua Sulis Minerva in Bath is a striking example. Among the various soldiers and settlers that arrived during the four-and-a-half centuries of Roman rule were followers of eastern religions such as Mithraism and Christianity.

The British church was well established by the fourth century. Christian martyrs had given their lives in witness to the risen Christ in the great Roman city of Verulamium (St Albans) and in the town of Caerleon on Usk. Some large houses contained chapels, frescoed with icons of the saints and with Christian symbols in their mosaic floors. Three British bishops were present at a church council in Arles early in the century, and the church was afflicted by the heresy of Arius, as was the rest of the Roman Empire. By the time Constantine was proclaimed Emperor in York in 312, there was as full a church life in Britain as in most other parts of the Empire.

The British writer Gildas depicts a church in the fifth and sixth centuries that is suffering from the ills associated with comfortable middle age. But there were British missionaries, most famously St Patrick in the fifth century. Others such as St Samson, St Beuno, St David, St Illtyd and St Petroc were active in Wales, Cornwall and Brittany. This mature church – with its bishops, martyrs, monastics, missionaries, its hermitages, monasteries, parish churches, liturgical traditions, relics and iconography – was part of the British world into which the Anglo-Saxon pagans were to arrive.

Very little is known about the Picts, and nearly every assertion made about them is open to challenge. Their lands were never part of the Roman Empire, and the great walls of Antoninus and Hadrian were built to keep them at bay. St Ninian, working from Whithorn in what is now south-west Scotland, was a fourth-century missionary to the Picts, and St Columba carried out a mission to the northern Picts in the sixth century. By Eanfled's time they were Christian, and southern Pictland was part of Northumbria for a time in the seventh century. This meant that Wilfrid, as Bishop of Northumbria, was responsible for Picts in the north of his diocese.

THE IRISH AND THEIR CHURCH

Irish influence in seventh-century Northumbria was profound. The relations between Ireland and Britain go back millennia, to the earliest use of the seaways between Ulster and Argyll, between Wexford and south-west Wales. E. G. Bowen[1] has demonstrated that the spread of Christianity from Iona to Northumbria followed ancient patterns of Irish cultural influence on its larger neighbour. But this influence went both ways and it was the British who were largely responsible for the conversion of Ireland.

The best-known British missionary is St Patrick, the priest's son snatched by pirates from Britain and sold into slavery in Ireland, later to return as a free man intent on winning his pagan masters for Christ. The evidence of churches dedicated to and therefore named after certain saints links St Patrick with Ulster, and his work was limited to north-east Ireland. The later tradition of St Patrick as the apostle of the whole of Ireland was the result of a successful propaganda campaign by the bishops of Armagh.

In fact there were Christians in the south of Ireland from early times. In 431 the Pope sent Bishop Palladius from Gaul to Ireland to organize an already existing church. Church dedications link this mission with Wicklow and with south-west Wales, and it is from Britain that the southern Irish received their Christianity and learned their Latin.

Having received their faith from Britain, the Irish church became the most flourishing part of western Christendom in the sixth century. People came to Ireland from all over Europe to pray and study in the numerous monasteries that stretched across the land. And Irish missionaries carried the faith across Europe, particularly to the Germanic kingdoms that had come into being after the collapse of Roman rule.

The northern coast of Ulster is close to the Hebrides and it was through Argyll that the return Irish mission to Britain took place. In 563 the 41-year-old Columba left his native Donegal to found a monastery on Iona, the tiny island off Mull. He was not leaving the Irish world, for these islands were part of the kingdom of Dalriata, formed by a people of north-east Ulster from around the River Bush. Dalriata was north of the British kingdom of Strathclyde and to the south-west of the land of the Picts.

In the seventh century the Irish are known by the name Scotti, or Scots. This term eventually came to refer only to the Irish settled in north Britain. When these Scots were eventually united with the Picts, the whole area became known as Scotland.

Columba's Iona became the centre of a major monastic commonwealth stretching from north Ireland, where daughter monasteries were founded at Derry and Durrow, to Pictland and Northumbria. It was in 616, half a century after its foundation, that the Northumbrian Prince Oswald came to live at this well-established and influential monastery.

THE GERMANIC TRIBES: ANGLES, SAXONS AND JUTES

The Germanic peoples settled in Britain in the fourth, fifth and sixth centuries. They came first as mercenaries and economic migrants, but increasingly as adversaries and invaders. The Welsh, Scots and Irish called them Saxons or 'Sassenachs'. The rest of the world now knows their descendants as English. Their origins are to be found among the tribal groups settled along the coasts of Scandinavia, North Germany and the Netherlands. Angles and Saxons formed the major groups and Anglo-Saxon is the term generally used to refer to them.

The nature of Anglo-Saxon settlements and the extent of the continuing British presence in the fifth and sixth centuries are matters of debate. The dominant view in the nineteenth century was that the 'ferocious Saxons' (the term used by the sixth-century

British writer Gildas) drove all before them and exterminated the British in the areas they controlled. At the other extreme is the view that the newcomers were agriculturalists, content to settle peacefully beside their British neighbours.

The picture is varied. The wide distribution of British place names is evidence that the British continued to inhabit many parts of the region of Britain now called England. The earliest Anglo-Saxon arrivals were probably Roman legionaries, some of whom settled after fulfilling their military term. In addition small war bands probably sailed across, established themselves on the east and south coasts and eventually made their way inland along the main waterways. In the fifth century a British leader recruited Saxons to repel the incursions of Scots and Picts. These soldiers, according to Gildas, then settled and later took possession of British lands by force. How and when the Anglo-Saxons wrested power from the British is not certain and presumably varied from place to place.

2

Northumbria in the Seventh Century

KING ETHELFRID CREATES NORTHUMBRIA

In the year 603 the pagan King Ethelfrid had inflicted a decisive defeat on the Irish kingdom of Dalriata. People from there never again seriously troubled the English tribes to the south. Ethelfrid was leader of the Bernicians, and he married into the neighbouring clan of Deira to unite the two peoples into one kingdom. Bernicia included modern Northumbria, and Deira modern Yorkshire.

Edwin, the successor to the leadership of the Deirans, fled to East Anglia where he was sheltered by King Redwald, known to us through the magnificent treasure, now in the British Museum, which was buried with him at Sutton Hoo.

Ethelfrid was at the height of his power when, in Bede's words, he 'ravaged the British more cruelly than all the other English leaders'. In 614 he pushed as far as Chester and defeated a British army, inflicting massive loss of life, including the massacre of 1,200 monks from the monastery of Bangor who were at prayer near the field of battle. With his northern neighbours defeated, the indigenous Britons subdued or driven to the west and potential rivals in exile, Ethelfrid's lands stretched from the River Humber to the Firth of Forth. This kingdom came to be known as Northumbria, the lands north of the Humber.

EANFLED'S FATHER, EDWIN, BECOMES KING (616)

Ethelfrid had sown the wind and he reaped the whirlwind. In 616 his brother-in-law Edwin defeated him on the banks of the River Idle, a tributary of the Trent in Mercian territory. Ethelfrid was killed on the battlefield. Now it was the turn of the Deiran Edwin to take over as King of Northumbria and for Ethelfrid's sons, Oswald and Oswy, to seek refuge, this time among the Scots and

Picts. The fact that Oswald found sanctuary on the island of Iona during his 17-year exile was the direct cause of the Irish mission to Northumbria.

Edwin was Eanfled's father. He ruled until 633, when he was defeated at the Battle of Hatfield near Doncaster by Cadwalla, the Christian King of Gwynedd, in alliance with the pagan King Penda of Mercia. Edwin and his sons were killed and the triumphant armies wrought vengeance on the Northumbrians. The throne fell to the exiled Bernician Oswald, who defeated Cadwalla one year later at the Battle of Heavenfield, not far from Hexham. This was in 634, the year of Wilfrid's birth. Oswald was to die eight years later in battle against the British. This was at Maserfelth, identified by most historians as Oswestry, or 'Oswald's Tree'.

The Battles of Chester, Dyrham (just north of Bath) and Oswestry played their part in establishing the western limits of Germanic power in relation to the British. Wales, the kingdoms of Rheged and Strathclyde, the Cornish peninsula and Man remained British, as did the Pennine kingdom of Elmet, centred on Leeds, until incorporated into Northumbria by King Edwin. Ethelfrid had eliminated the Irish as a political presence south of the Antonine Wall. The line between Scots and Picts was constantly shifting; that between Northumbrian Angles and Picts finally settled at the Clyde–Forth line after the English defeat at Dunnichen Moss in 685, a battle that was to be one of the turning points in Wilfrid's life.

Dynastic marriage, treaty and the allegiance of minor kingdoms all played their part in the ever-shifting balance of power. But such matters were more normally settled by bloodshed. Kings usually died in battle. Only two Northumbrian kings in the seventh century died a natural death. Three died in battle against close relatives. One was murdered. Another fought against his father and disappeared without trace. Egfrid, who had carried out a barbarous massacre in Ireland, finally fell to the Picts. A similar story could be told for the other Anglo-Saxon kingdoms. The table of Battles and Succession to the Northumbrian Throne on p. vii lists the main battles that affected the succession of the Northumbrian kings.

It was in this world of political change, internecine strife and warfare that most of the English became Christian. All the Anglo-

Saxon kingdoms, if not all their people, were pagan in 597, the year when St Columba died on Iona and St Augustine arrived in Canterbury. By the end of the seventh century, all had adopted Christianity.

The map on p. xi shows the patchwork complexity of Britain's political geography at the time of Wilfrid's birth, by which time the Germanic peoples were established in more or less defined tribal kingdoms. These often followed the boundaries of the earlier British kingdoms and sometimes retained Celtic names, as with Bernicia, Deira and Kent. East Anglia and the kingdoms of the West Saxons, East Saxons and South Saxons were named after the ethnic origin of the newcomers. Mercia was so called because it included the Marches or boundary lands. Wilfrid was to be active in all these kingdoms apart from East Anglia and Essex.

3

The Coming of Christianity to the Northumbrian Angles

There were three ways in which the Angles of Northumbria encountered the Church in the seventh century: first, from the indigenous Britons; second, from the Christians who accompanied Ethelberga, the daughter of the Kentish king, when she came to be married to King Edwin; and third from the Irish of Iona.

THE BRITISH INFLUENCE

Our sources do not tell us of a British mission. In fact Bede frequently castigates the British for their failure to preach to the English when their Germanic ancestors first arrived, and most historians follow him in believing that their role in the conversion of the Anglo-Saxons was negligible, if not non-existent.

There were doubtless bitter memories of the warfare of the first half of the seventh century between the Northumbrian Angles and the British, who were often allied to Mercia, which was Northumbria's rival for superiority in the Anglo-Saxon world. Many of the British who fled before the Northumbrian sword would have seen their churches taken over by the newly converted English. It would not have been easy for them to regard such people as brothers and sisters in Christ. Some harboured resentment for many years. We know of some British Christians at the beginning of the eighth century who refused even to eat with English Christians, and destroyed any crockery touched by them.

But there were long periods of peace, particularly during the reign of Edwin, when the two peoples lived side by side. The English of the Severn valley became Christian through unremarkable and unrecorded day-to-day contacts with their British neighbours. This must also have happened in Northumbria.

Edwin was the first of the Northumbrian kings to be baptized. As we have noted, he married Ethelberga, the daughter of the Christian king of Kent, and she had come north on the understanding that she would be able to practise her Christian faith. She was therefore accompanied by one of Pope Gregory the Great's Kentish missionaries, Bishop Paulinus. The marriage took place in July 625, and at Easter the following year a daughter, Eanfled, was born.

Before adopting the Christian faith himself, Edwin had to consider the political consequences. It could work to his advantage in the complex diplomatic world of Britain with its indigenous Christian population, its numerous Anglo-Saxon kingdoms and sub-kingdoms and ever-changing clan allegiances. But Bede tells us that Edwin was a serious and thoughtful person who 'often sat alone for long periods in silence . . . deliberating with himself what he ought to do and which religion he should adhere to'.

Two of Bede's most engrossing stories throw light on the complexity and seriousness of the king's deliberations. Edwin was discussing his religious affiliation with his chief men when one of them told a parable. He likened human life to the flight of a sparrow that comes out of the wintry storms into the royal hall, with its warm fire and bright light, and then flits out again into the cold and dark. The bright warmth of the mead hall is a fleeting interlude before the dark unknown of death. The gospel of the resurrection gave more certain knowledge. The cold, wintry world of Grendel and other dark demons of Anglo-Saxon legend could be bathed in the warmth of the eternal light of the risen Christ.

Bede's other story is the account of the frightening appearance of an unnamed stranger to Edwin in the middle of the night. Edwin was in exile in East Anglia and was sitting 'in silent anguish of spirit', expecting to be murdered at any moment by assassins sent by King Ethelfrid. The stranger asked him what reward he would give the man who could free him from his troubles. Edwin replied that he would give him anything in his power. The stranger then asked if he would follow this man's advice if 'he gave wiser guidance for your life and salvation than anything known to your parents and kinsfolk'. Edwin promised. The stranger then placed his right hand upon his head and said: 'When you receive this sign, remember this occasion.'

One day, when he was king, Edwin was pondering the question of religion. As he sat in reflection, Bishop Paulinus appeared and laid his right hand upon his head and asked if he remembered the sign. Eventually, the king was baptized in the newly built wooden church of St Peter in York in 627. This is the tradition of his baptism as recorded by Bede.

But there is an alternative, British tradition of Edwin's reception into the Church. According to this story, he spent time in exile in Anglesey and was baptized by Rhun, one of the leading figures in the British kingdom of Rheged. So Edwin was baptized by one of the 'Men of the North', as the Welsh called their fellow Britons in Rheged. This tradition is recorded in the Welsh Annals and by Nennius, the eighth-century British historian, but is not mentioned by Bede.

The baptism could have been carried out jointly by Paulinus and Rhun, as Keith Jackson[2] suggests, but it is also possible that Paulinus' baptism was the 'completion' expected of British baptism by those of the Roman tradition. These two traditions of Edwin's baptism, the English and the British, reflect the reality that there were both British and Kentish influences at work in the conversion of the Northumbrians.

THE IRISH MISSION

The third, and most profound, source of the Christian faith for the Northumbrian Angles started to flow only on the death of Edwin and the succession of the Ionan-educated Oswald. As soon as he became king, Oswald called on Iona to send someone to instruct his fellow Angles, and Aidan was the Irish monk who came. He drew many to Christ through his fervour and humility, and in 634 he and Oswald founded the monastery at Lindisfarne, which was to become the heart of Northumbrian Christianity. It was here that the teenage Wilfrid had his first experience of the monastic life.

Aidan arrived in Northumbria without a knowledge of Anglo-Saxon, and in the early days King Oswald would interpret for him.

In time, the Irish became bilingual and some of the English monks became fluent in Irish. Many Angles retained a great love for Irish ways and carried Ionan Christianity well beyond the boundaries of Northumbria. Chad, who was active in Mercia, and his brother Cedd, who brought Christianity to Essex, are two of the more striking examples. Wilfrid, who is often portrayed as an opponent of the Irish, is a more complex example of the same tradition.

Notes

1 E. G. Bowen, *Saints, Seaways and Settlements in the Celtic Lands.* University of Wales, Cardiff, 1969.
2 K. Jackson, 'The North British Section in Nennius', in N. Jackson and N. K. Chadwick, *Celt and Saxon.* Cambridge University Press, 1963.

Part II

Grounding and Growth in the Christian Life

4

The Three Women in Wilfrid's Early Life

Wilfrid was born in Northumbria in 634, the year that Oswald succeeded to the throne, following his victory over Mercia and the British, who had defeated and killed King Edwin the year before. The names and background of Wilfrid's parents are unknown to us. But we do know that his father was of the nobility and was close to the king. He might well have given service to Edwin and Oswald, as well as Oswy, who became king in Wilfrid's eighth year.

It appears that Wilfrid was a devoted son, for he was vigorously active in his father's household. With self-effacing grace he moved among the mead benches of the great hall to serve his father's guests, including companions of the king. Wilfrid's father was a man of standing to be on good terms with those close to the king, and his son was at home among the Anglo-Saxon aristocracy. Their values of integrity, honour, courage, loyalty, eloquence and open-hearted generosity were his values; the political complexities of their world were familiar to him, as were the heroism and brutality of their battlefields.

Wilfrid also served the servants of his father's guests. He was a servant of the servants. To grasp this crucial feature in Wilfrid's early life is to understand the springs of his inspiration, at once Anglo-Saxon and profoundly Christian.

The Anglo-Saxon epic poem, *Beowulf*, was written to celebrate the battle-hardened skills, strength, courage and eloquence of a great hero. But these qualities have their lasting significance because Beowulf devoted them to the service of his people. His gigantic struggle with the demonic Grendel, and his descent into the depths of the cold lake to destroy Grendel's gruesome mother, gain their dramatic power in the conquest that saved his people from the ravages of these evil demons. In old age, Beowulf was to meet his death in a conflict on behalf of his people. His struggles were for all of his people, high-born and lowly. In the feast that followed his triumph, his queen served the least and the greatest with equal grace.

Such stories were part of Wilfrid's world. For the Christian, they are pagan intimations of a deeper truth, that Christ, the Son of God, the son of Man, came 'not to be served, but to serve and to give his life as a ransom for many'. This was the king in whose kingdom Wilfrid wished to serve: the Master who wrapped a towel around his waist and stooped to wash his followers' feet; the Saviour who died for his people on the cross; the King who descended into the depths of Hades, destroyed death, bound the devil and brought life to all.

The young Wilfrid had, so his biographer Eddius tells us, 'none of the fads common to boys', and he never wavered in his early commitment to the kingdom of God. In this we surely see the influence of his very devout (*valde religiosa*) mother.

WILFRID'S MOTHER

We can only speculate on the sources of his mother's piety. Perhaps she came from an established Anglo-British family with roots in the early Christianity of the area before the arrival of the Angles. As the family was close to King Oswy, who had been nurtured during his exile in the ways of the Irish church, Wilfrid's parents would have been influenced by this, perhaps even brought up in the same tradition. Another possibility is that Wilfrid's parents were baptized by Paulinus, the bishop who accompanied Eanfled's mother, Ethelberga, from Kent when she came to marry King Edwin in Northumbria. Wilfrid's mother might even have been among the Christian companions of Ethelberga. If this were the case, it would explain the ease of Wilfrid's access to her daughter.

Whatever its immediate origin, the Christian faith of Wilfrid's parents appears to have been profound. His mother was evidently the vital influence in his formation. But we also know that his father supported Wilfrid in his ambition to give himself to the service of God, for he readily gave his blessing for him to leave home and present his request to the queen. The story here may be more complicated for, at some stage, his mother died and we hear of a 'harsh, cruel' stepmother.

WILFRID'S STEPMOTHER

The cruel stepmother is a stereotype of the fairy tale; she was a reality among the Germanic royalty of this time. As there was no law of primogeniture, according to which the first son succeeded the father, all male relatives had a claim to succession, and this created mistrust between brothers, cousins and uncles, and not least between stepmothers and stepsons. In his *History of the Franks*, St Gregory of Tours tells us that it was customary for stepmothers to maltreat their stepsons, and he related a story in which a stepmother had her stepson murdered. Sons of a first wife were a threat not only to the children of the second wife, but to the security of the stepmother herself. It is not impossible that Wilfrid's stepmother had made it a condition of her marriage that the 'threat' of Wilfrid be removed.

At 14 he was old enough for military service to the king, and this may be one reason why he sought royal protection for the path he had chosen. The queen's support could also have been impor-tant in helping him to confront possible problems from his stepmother. It is difficult to know about the emotional expecta-tions of a young Anglo-Saxon aristocrat but, in a world where ties of kinship were highly revered, it is likely that the security of a substitute kinship would have been an additional reason for Wilfrid to seek the 'protection' of the queen.

It was not only a blessing that Wilfrid's father gave him when he left home. He made sure that his son came before Queen Eanfled nobly dressed and accompanied, as if he had been despatched to serve at the court. He also appeared before her with the recommendations of those companions of the king whom he had so well served in his father's house. The trappings and recommendations doubtless played their part, but Queen Eanfled was taken by the personal qualities of this open and driven young man.

It may be that women have a more profound influence on the continuity of tradition than their menfolk, particularly when the men die early in battle. Certainly, Queen Eanfled played a major part in the political and ecclesiastical developments of her time, a part that is understated in our sources.

QUEEN EANFLED AND HER FAMILY

Eanfled was born on the holy night of Easter in 626. Earlier in the day, her father King Edwin had narrowly escaped death. An assassin from the court of the West Saxons attempted to run him through with his double-edged and poison-tipped sword, but a thegn threw himself before his king. The thegn was killed and the wounded Edwin made a vow that, if God would grant him life and victory over the king who had sent the assassin, he would 'renounce his idols and serve Christ'. Seven weeks later, on the feast of Pentecost, perhaps while her father was waging his successful campaign against the West Saxons, Eanfled was baptized.

Eanfled had a Northumbrian father, but her mother's mother came from the Frankish royal family whose capital was Paris. The Franks were a Germanic tribe that had taken control of northern Gaul and ultimately gave their name to the country. They had adopted Christianity a generation before the Anglo-Saxons and Eanfled's grandmother, Bertha, had grown up a devout Christian.

There were many contacts between the Franks and the Germanic settlers in Kent and it was Bertha's destiny to create closer ties by making a dynastic marriage to the Kentish King Ethelbert. But he and his people were pagans and Bertha was not prepared to compromise. She made it a condition of her marriage that she should be able to continue to practise her Christian faith, and arrived in Kent accompanied by her own bishop.

Bertha used to worship in the British-built church dedicated to St Martin in the east of Canterbury, and it is likely that her fellow-worshippers included indigenous Britons whose Christianity dated back to the earliest centuries. When Augustine arrived from Rome on his mission to the English, he came to an existing Christian community that had full royal approval. He baptized King Ethelbert, but much of the work of winning him had already been done by his wife Bertha.

The daughter of this marriage, Ethelberga, was Eanfled's mother. She was brought up in a Christian tradition that blended the practices of Frankish Gaul with those of Rome, on the foundations of the British church. She was the daughter of the first Christian king of Kent and grew up in Canterbury, which was to become the seat of the archbishop.

Ethelberga, like her mother, made a dynastic marriage. Her marriage to Edwin linked Kent to Northumbria. Edwin may have been baptized already, but he clearly was still debating the question of his faith. Ethelberga's bishop, Paulinus, completed his baptism and also baptized Eanfled.

THE BATTLE OF HATFIELD CHASE 633

When Eanfled was only seven, her father and two of her half-brothers were killed in the Battle of Hatfield Chase and it became too dangerous for the family to stay in Northumbria. Her mother, Ethelberga, returned home to Kent, taking her two small children and some of the extended family with her. They made the journey by sea under the protection of Bass, a brave thegn of the king, and were accompanied by Bishop Paulinus and other members of the queen's Christian retinue who had come north with her on her marriage eight years earlier.

The following year Oswald succeeded to the Northumbrian throne, and it was no longer safe for Eanfled's infant brother nor for her nephew, the young son of her recently killed half-brother, to remain in Britain. As male members of the family, they were potential claimants to the throne, so they were sent abroad to stay with a relative, the Frankish King Dagobert I. Both of them died in infancy. Ethelberga's place in her daughter's life was made more than usually important by these drastic events.

Both in her first seven years in Northumbria and during the years in Kent where she reached maturity, Eanfled had therefore grown up in the Christian tradition of her mother and grand-mother. She remained in Kent until she became betrothed to Edwin's successor to the Northumbrian throne, Oswy. He became king in 642 following Oswald's death on the battlefield at Oswestry.

An Irish priest named Utta, who later became Abbot of Gateshead, was sent to accompany Eanfled on her journey from Kent to Oswy's court. They travelled by sea and were caught up in a terrifying storm. The boat was foundering and all were preparing for their last moments, when Utta poured holy oil on to the wild waves and the storm was stilled. The oil had been given to him by Aidan. So Eanfled returned to her birthplace under the protection of the great Irish missionary to the Angles of the north. Nurtured in a Christianity whose customs were Gallic, Roman and British, she first encountered the Christian traditions of Ireland on this sea journey.

This introduction was important, for things had changed since her early childhood. The mission of Aidan and the founding of Lindisfarne meant that Irish customs were now dominant in Northumbria. However, Eanfled had come north with her own priest, Romanus, and continued in the traditions in which she had been raised by her mother.

The fundamentals of the faith were, of course, the same as those held by the Irish; the differences had to do with local customs, of which the most obvious was the date of Easter. King Oswy kept the Irish date and Queen Eanfled the Alexandrian date that had been recently adopted by Rome.

EANFLED AND NORTHUMBRIAN POLITICS: RIVALRY BETWEEN DEIRA AND BERNICIA

The marriage of Eanfled, daughter of the Deiran King Edwin, to Oswy the Bernician, formed part of the policy of uniting these two kingdoms, a policy that was never wholly successful. Although Oswy's reign lasted 28 years, its stability was constantly threatened by Deiran opposition. He made members of his own family sub-kings of Deira, but even they turned against him. The underlying tension between Deira and Bernicia was one of the constant political realities faced by the new queen.

For the first seven years of Oswy's reign, Eanfled's second cousin Oswin was sub-king of Deira. He was renowned for his piety and Christian faith. He once gave a fine horse to Aidan, who promptly gave it away to the first beggar he met. When challenged by the king, Aidan asked, 'Surely this son of a mare is not dearer to you than that son of God?' King Oswin, who had just come in from hunting, was warming himself by the fire. After a time he suddenly threw himself at Aidan's feet declaring that never again would he question how his gifts were used. During the evening Aidan became very sad and, when questioned, answered, 'I know that the King will not live long; for I never before saw a meek king.' His prophecy was fulfilled. Oswy, the Bernician, had Oswin, the Deiran, murdered.

Eanfled was able to exact some recompense from her husband for this murder of her cousin. In answer to her request, Oswy gave land at Gilling, near Oswaldkirk, the place of Oswin's murder, for a monastery at which prayers could be said both for the murderer and for his victim. The first abbot was Trumhere, who was an Angle and a relative of Oswin. He had been educated in Ireland, and later became Bishop of Mercia. And it was at Gilling that Ceolfrid, Bede's beloved abbot, served his novitiate. The monastery of Gilling is a good example of the close interchange between Irish, Anglian and Kentish traditions.

EANFLED'S DAUGHTER AND THE WAR WITH MERCIA

The murder of Oswin did not remove Oswy's dynastic problems. He gave the sub-kingship of Deira to his nephew Ethelwald, Oswald's son, but rather than remaining loyal to his uncle, Ethelwald allied himself with Penda of Mercia, the long-standing enemy of Northumbria.

Penda was intent on 'wiping out the entire nation from the highest to the humblest'. He had formed a powerful alliance with the East Angles and had 30 experienced commanders with all their troops on his side. Oswy's forces were greatly outnumbered and he attempted to reach a peaceful settlement with Penda by offering him gifts. These were turned down. He therefore vowed to make offerings to God if he were granted victory. The most precious of these gifts was Eanfled's daughter, the tiny one-year-old Aelffled, who was to be 'consecrated to God in perpetual virginity'. Oswy also vowed to grant land for the building of monasteries.

In 655 Oswy had an amazing victory over Penda, at a battle fought on the River Winwaed, a tributary of the Humber. Virtually all of Penda's great commanders were killed and many of his men were drowned in the swollen waters of the flooded river. Oswy concluded his successful campaign at Leeds. His son Alchfrid fought alongside him and was made sub-king of Deira in place of his treacherous cousin. Alchfrid became a close friend of Wilfrid and helped to establish him in Deira.

EANFLED, THE DEVOUT AND POWERFUL QUEEN

As he had promised, Oswy gave land for the building and support of six monasteries in Deira and six in Bernicia, and the baby Aelffled was consecrated to God. She later served her novitiate under the Abbess Hilda at Hartlepool, followed her to Whitby and eventually became abbess in her turn. In her old age, the widowed Eanfled became joint abbess with her daughter, and it was at Whitby that they both died and were buried.

The offspring of a dynastic marriage, born the day of an assassination attempt on her father, Eanfled – the half-Deiran, quarter-Kentish, quarter-Frankish princess – married her cousin Oswy, himself the son of a Bernician-Deiran alliance. Her father, her husband, her cousins and sons were all involved in political alliances, intrigue and warfare. Her husband was one of the few not to die by the sword. She founded monasteries, brought peoples to Christ and concluded her days in this world as Abbess of Whitby. It was to this experienced, devout, powerful and widely connected woman of the world that the motherless Wilfrid turned for advice and protection in 648. He was 14 and she was 22.

When he came to the queen, Wilfrid was not specific about the service he would like to give; that was left to her. Her decision is striking. One of the king's most devoted companions was a certain Cudda, who was so physically disabled that he had abandoned his worldly ambitions and resolved to dedicate himself to the monastic life. Queen Eanfled commended Wilfrid to act as his servant and to join him in the monastery of Lindisfarne. This he did with total dedication for the next four years.

5

Wilfrid's First Years in the Monastery (648–652)

❧

By the age of 14 Wilfrid had a good grounding in the Christian faith. Coming from a devout family, he would have been familiar with the Scriptures, with the daily and weekly pattern of services, the annual cycle of festivals and the sacramental life of the Church. All the biblical and liturgical texts were in Latin, so he would have had at least a reasonable acquaintance with the language and, given his ready intelligence and his social background, he might well have had a thorough grounding in it. At Lindisfarne he entered a great centre of Christian life and learning.

LINDISFARNE

Founded by St Aidan at the time of Wilfrid's birth, Lindisfarne, though a young monastery, had all the resources of Iona to draw upon. Aidan and his fellow Irish monks were deeply versed in the monastic life and would have brought with them manuscripts, icons and a sound knowledge of the Scriptures, the canons of the Church and its liturgical and musical tradition. For a number of years Wilfrid was steeped in this rich tradition of Irish Christianity. Ireland was renowned for its Christian learning throughout western Christendom at this time. We hear of devout people from Gaul and Britain travelling there to spend years studying in the monasteries, some of them to return and become church leaders in their own lands.

The great missionary movement from Ireland had begun in the sixth century. The most famous examples of this are the two saints Columbanus and Columba, both named after the dove and noted for their ascetic life, but both men of authority and deep learning. Columbanus' mission was to the Franks of Gaul and the Lombards of north Italy; Columba's to the Picts. By the time Wilfrid embarked on his life of monastic discipline and learning, there was no need for him to travel to Ireland; the Irish had come to his native Northumbria and it was in an Irish monastery that he received his first education as a monk.

In the peace of Lindisfarne, Wilfrid worked as the servant of the disabled Cudda, a job he carried out 'with heartfelt zeal'. So he continued his life of serving others. This and the humble and obedient way in which he carried out the rule of the monastery endeared him not only to Cudda but to all the monks. The older ones regarded him as a son and the younger ones as a brother. His home life of Christian obedience continued naturally in the monastery. Despite his many travels and the great responsibilities he was later to take on as bishop, the monastery remained his natural home for the rest of his life.

WILFRID'S EDUCATION

Common to all monastic life was a disciplined pattern of prayer and a thorough knowledge of the Scriptures, particularly the psalms, which were known by heart and formed the basis of vespers, nocturns, matins, the first, third, sixth and ninth hours and compline, which together made up the daily office. Of direct significance for Lindisfarne was the example of Aidan. 'All who walked with him,' said Bede, 'whether monks or lay-folk, were required to meditate; that is, either to read the Scriptures or to learn the psalms. This was their daily occupation, wherever they went.' We find Wilfrid following this example during his travels.

So biblical learning would have formed the basis of Wilfrid's education. We do not hear any details of the other sides of young Wilfrid's education in the monastery, but it is likely to have been similar to that of St Columbanus, whose biographer tells us about his schooling. As a boy in Leinster he studied letters and the work of the grammarians, 'as befitted a freeman'. He then progressed to the study of the Holy Scriptures in the monastery of Bangor, one of the great family of monasteries of Ulster. This thorough grounding in the Latin language doubtless followed the classical patterns that included 'grammar' and 'rhetoric' and enabled the student to read fluently and to express his ideas in speech and writing. Columbanus wrote a commentary on the psalms in a distinguished Latin style, and Wilfrid learned all the psalms by heart as well as several other books. Later Wilfrid was to become word-perfect in the Gospels, and he would surely have learnt great sections of them while at Lindisfarne.

Wilfrid's first encounter with monastic life was in the Irish tradition. Had it been in Greece, Egypt, Rome or Syria he would have had fundamentally the same experience. But it was very important that he did have the chance to become thoroughly acquainted with the traditions of St Columba, which were so fundamental to the Northumbrian church. Aidan died in 651, three years after Wilfrid entered the monastery, so Wilfrid is likely to have known him and other leaders of the Irish mission, some of whom he might already have encountered in his father's house.

WILFRID DECIDES TO VISIT ROME

After a few years Wilfrid developed a longing to go on a pilgrimage to Rome. This was a natural aspiration for someone living among the Irish, for whom Rome held a strong attraction. Eddius observes that 'it was a road hitherto untravelled by our people', meaning the English, but they too developed a similar tradition in time. The tombs of the martyrs were the goal of pilgrimage from the earliest times. Rome, as the only apostolic see in the west and the place of martyrdom of both St Peter and St Paul, was a natural focus for devotion.

Bede says that, being a thoughtful youth, he realized that the ways of the Irish were 'far from perfect' (*minime perfectam*) and that this was the reason for his wish to go to Rome. If this were the reason, it is strange that Eddius, who never misses the chance to upbraid the Irish, does not mention it. What is certain is that Wilfrid would have been familiar with the differences in practice between the two traditions. There were remnants of the Canterbury mission among the communities brought to Christ by the Ionan mission, and Queen Eanfled continued with her Kentish customs at the court. The question of the date of Easter, was a live issue in Ireland itself. There had been concern in the south of the country that there was a difference over the date of Easter and a delegation visited Rome to see things for themselves. Here they discovered that the whole Christian world had the same date for Easter, which was different from the day kept in Ireland. Shortly after their return, the churches in the south of Ireland adopted the 'Roman' date. This had happened in 635, when Wilfrid was one year old.

One of these southern Irish delegates, Ronan, visited Lindisfarne and raised the matter with Abbot Finan, who succeeded Aidan. Finan strongly resisted any change. This meeting probably took place shortly after Wilfrid had left Lindisfarne, but clearly the issue was a matter of hot debate at this time. It might well have been an additional reason why a young man of enquiring mind should want to go to Rome and see it for himself.

Cudda understood at once the genuineness of Wilfrid's wish, as did the elders of the monastery. They gave their blessing for him to go and Cudda informed Queen Eanfled, whose guidance and support once again played a vital part. She equipped Wilfrid handsomely for the journey and sent him, with the highest commendations, to her cousin Erconbert, the King of Kent, there to await suitable fellow-travellers.

6

The First Journey to Rome (653–656)

Canterbury was an important centre of Christian life in Britain. In Wilfrid's lifetime, under the great Syrian Greek Archbishop Theodore, it was to become the most important seat of learning in western Christendom. Wilfrid was to spend a year here and would have met the second and third generations of the mission sent by St Gregory the Great. He would have become familiar with the tradition in which his mentor and protector Queen Eanfled had been raised by her mother with its Gallic, Frankish, Roman and British elements.

Wilfrid spent a year in Kent; according to Eddius one 'of tedious waiting'. Given his goal, there must have been some frustration. But here, as in all his many travels, he lived a life of 'prayer, fasting, vigils and reading'; the Irish-trained novice was immediately at home in the 'Roman' world of Kent. It was the same Christian world with its full liturgical life and its local customs and practices; those minor variations that give a richness to the Christian experience. He also continued his studies. Previously he had used St Jerome's version of the psalms; 'Now he learnt by heart the fifth edition, the one in use in Rome.' Given his activities, it is certain that his time was spent in a monastery.

The Kentish king appeared to be in no hurry to send Wilfrid on his journey. He had an obligation to protect him and he 'came to love him dearly' when he saw his devotion. Perhaps he wanted this exceptional young man to contribute to the life of his kingdom. But Eanfled continued to take a direct interest in her protégé and prompted the king to find a suitable guide and companion for his journey to Rome. The person he found was Benedict Baducing, usually known as Benedict Biscop.

Benedict Biscop was one of the most remarkable of the Northumbrian Angles. He came from a noble family but, at the age of 25, he abandoned the life of military leadership to become a monk. He founded sister monasteries on the river Tyne, the first at Wearmouth dedicated to St Peter and the second at Jarrow, dedicated to St Paul. He was a great traveller to the Mediterranean world, where he gathered what was needed for his new monasteries. He collected books, icons and relics. He persuaded both cantors and icon-painters to come to Northumbria and teach his monks.

Biscop created one of the West's great libraries. It was in this library that Bede gained his encyclopaedic knowledge. He and others got to know the writings of the early fathers of the Church and passed on this tradition through their preaching and teaching. The scriptorium on the Tyne produced great illuminated manuscripts, including the one now known to the world as the Codex Amiatinus, which was sent as a present to the Pope of Rome and is now preserved in the library in Florence. Biscop made it his business to visit many monasteries on the continent and to study their rule of life so that Wearmouth and Jarrow could draw from their experience.

There is no evidence of any particular warmth in the relationship between Biscop and Wilfrid. But Wilfrid must have learnt much from his 'austere guide', as Eddius calls him, and he was later to follow his example and enrich his own churches in Ripon, York and Hexham with gifts brought back from his continental travels. Biscop accompanied Wilfrid as far as Lyon, stayed with him there for some time, but then continued on his way, leaving Wilfrid with the local bishop, Annemund.[1]

WILFRID IS OFFERED A WIFE

Bishop Annemund took an immediate liking to Wilfrid, seeing a quality of saintliness in him, and treated him as one of his own family. 'Stay with me and be trustful,' he said, 'and I shall give you a good part of Gaul to govern in perpetuity and my own niece to be your wife. I shall adopt you as my son and you shall have me as a father and faithful helper in all things.' The immediate impact that Wilfrid made on Annemund testifies to Wilfrid's human warmth, to his lively and sensitive intelligence, to his clarity and genuineness of purpose; those very qualities that had endeared him to Eanfled, to Cudda and the monks of Lindisfarne and to King Erconbert of Kent.

Wilfrid's response to this extraordinary offer is very telling: 'I have made my vows to the Lord', he said, 'leaving, like Abraham, my kinsfolk and my father's house to visit the Apostolic See, there to learn the laws of ecclesiastical discipline so that our nation may grow in the service of God. If with God's help I am still alive, I promise to come back to see you.'

Not only did Wilfrid come back to see him, but he also spent a further three years with his 'father' Annemund on his return. These years in Lyon were to be the most formative for his knowledge of the order and practice of the Church and especially for his understanding of the work of a bishop. Before looking at this, let us accompany him to Rome.

ROME, CITY OF REFUGEES AND EXILES

The Persian invasions of the Holy Land (they took Jerusalem in 614) led to a large number of Syrian, Palestinian and Greek exiles seeking refuge in Rome, where they established monasteries and other institutions. Rome became a place of great ethnic and linguistic diversity, with a variety of liturgical and ecclesiastical traditions. Further exiles settled there, following the Muslim Arab conquests in the Near East. In 641 a Greek from Jerusalem became pope, and from this time to the end of Wilfrid's life many of the popes were Greek or Syrian. Greek elements were introduced into the Roman liturgy, and Byzantine iconographers were active in the churches of Rome, many of which were being built or renewed at this time.

There were also theological exiles from the East. In his attempts to reconcile the Monophysite[2] Christians of Egypt and gain their support in his conflicts with the Persians and Arabs, the Emperor Heraclius got himself involved in theology. Heraclius and his successors attempted to impose an unorthodox, compromise doctrine known as Monothelitism[3] on the Church, and persecuted their Orthodox opponents. One of these was the greatest theologian of the seventh century, Maximus the Confessor. Almost certainly in Rome at the same time as Wilfrid, he was captured there in 655 by soldiers from the emperor and sent to die in exile with his tongue and right hand cut off. A church council had met in the Lateran and condemned the heretical doctrines of the emperor. The pope who chaired this meeting was called Martin. He was unjustly tried for treason and, at the time of Wilfrid's visit, was dying of cold and neglect, exiled in the Crimea.

THE POPES AS BUILDERS

Italy had been devastated by foreign invasions in the sixth century, and these were followed by famine and sickness. Gregory the Great had given all his family wealth to the relief of suffering. In the absence of any political leaders, he devoted his enormous administrative abilities to the management of affairs. He established a robust administration to care for the poor, the orphaned and the destitute. This was in addition to his active interest in the liturgical and monastic life of Rome and the development of the Church's mission. He established a tradition of strong leadership by the pope so that the bishop of seventh-century Rome had considerable authority and influence.

Many of the seventh-century popes used their position to create impressive buildings. New churches were built, such as the one dedicated to St Pancras. St Peter's was refurbished and had major work done to the roof. Great secular buildings like the Senate house were converted into churches. From the ruins of war, Rome was rising as an imposing and more Christian city. Much of the architecture and iconography of these new buildings was the work of Byzantine artists. The Christian mosaics, arches and domes of Rome came to match those of Ravenna and Constantinople.

All this would have been absorbed by the young pilgrim Wilfrid as he travelled on his daily visits to the shrines of the saints. He had a particular devotion to the apostle Andrew and prayed each day in the chapel dedicated to him. Wherever he could, he collected relics of the saints to take back with him to Northumbria.

On one of his visits Wilfrid met Boniface, an archdeacon 'sent by God and the apostle'. Boniface became his faithful friend and teacher. He first made him word-perfect in the four Gospels and then gave him a thorough grounding in canon law and church matters. At the conclusion of his studies, Boniface presented Wilfrid to the pope who, having learnt the purpose of his visit, gave him his blessing. Uncharacteristically, Eddius does not tell us the name of this pope. It is very likely to have been Eugenius, who was installed during Martin's exile. His uncanonical appointment could explain Eddius' silence.

It was natural that Wilfrid had gone to Rome as a pilgrim to the place of the martyrdom of the apostles Peter and Paul, and to learn about church affairs at the centre of western Christendom. But he would have drunk in many other things: the grandeur of church architecture and iconography; the rich and developing nature of the liturgy; the vitality of eastern monastic life; the power and authority of the bishops, who ruled in the best traditions of a traditional governor of the Roman Empire, caring for their people and creating great buildings in which to glorify God. In the lives of Maximus the Confessor and Pope Martin he had encountered living examples of martyrdom, of those who would rather face death than compromise their faith. He would deepen his experience of these things on his return to Lyon.

7

Lyon (656–659)

At Rome, Wilfrid had the benefit of a learned teacher. At Lyon he not only had 'learned tutors'; he was part of the bishop's household and was able to experience at first hand an ancient and great diocese, with its many buildings, its great library, its large scriptoria and its tradition of learning in canon law. This is why Lyon, where he spent so much time, is central to his development. To understand him, we need to know something of the church of Lyon.

THE EARLY MARTYRS OF LYON

The church of the early centuries spread first through the Greek-speaking cities of the Mediterranean world. Southern Gaul had ancient Greek settlements and the early church in Lyon had particular connections with Asia Minor. It was from there that their famous bishop St Irenaeus came, and it was to the churches of Asia and Phrygia that one of the most powerful and moving accounts of early Christian martyrdom was sent.

The martyrs of Lyon and Vienne were hunted out of their houses in 177. They suffered the full panoply of torture; then, abused and battered, they were dragged before the howling mob in the amphitheatre to be torn by wild beasts and thrown into a red-hot chair that stood in its centre. The martyr Sanctus, his limbs horribly swollen and inflamed from his torture, replied to all the questions of the judge with the simple words, 'I am a Christian.' The small woman Blandina was beaten and slashed mercilessly from dawn till dusk, till her torturers were exhausted. Nevertheless they extracted no denial of Christ from her but only the words: 'I am a Christian and with us no evil finds a place.' She was then suspended on a stake before the mob as food for the beasts. Here she hung cross-wise in earnest prayer, giving courage to others who saw 'in the form of their sister, Him who was crucified for them'. Hundreds were stretched in the stocks in prison, lying in their filth, trampled on and left to die. Their bodies were then thrown as food to the dogs.[4]

Bishop Pothinus, over 90 years old and weakened by sickness, had the joy of confessing Christ before the governor, to the fury of the crowd who kicked and punched him and hailed him with whatever missiles came to hand. Thrown into prison, he died two days later. The remains of the martyrs were incinerated and the ashes thrown into the River Rhone in the hope of destroying any faith in their resurrection, the belief in which had given them great courage in the face of suffering and joy in the face of death.

THE BISHOPS OF LYON

These early martyrs of Lyon are commemorated to this day in the Church. Their memory would have been a vivid inspiration in seventh-century Lyon. Bishop Pothinus was not the only bishop of Lyon to be martyred, so too was his successor Irenaeus, mentioned above, the great theologian of the early church. Wilfrid was to discover, before he left Lyon, that the tradition of martyred bishops lived on to his day.

Gaul had been more fully integrated into the Roman Empire than Britain. The nobles in its indigenous Celtic population rose to leading positions, creating a Gallo-Roman aristocracy thoroughly imbued with the patrician virtues of Rome. The Germanic invasions – of Burgundians in the south and Franks in the north – did not destroy them and the government of Lyon and the other cities continued in the hands of this traditional aristocracy. Lyon was the seat of a metropolitan bishop, who was himself nearly always drawn from their number and eventually became their most powerful representative.

The ideal Roman governor was devout, learned, eloquent and disciplined. Above all, he would show a fatherly care for his people, expressed in the dispassionate hearing of lawsuits and in abundant generosity towards those in need. These Roman virtues were also those of the best of the bishops, both in Lyon and Rome. The fifth-century Bishop Patiens, for example, fed thousands of people at his own expense during a famine that followed an invasion of the Goths.

It was the Christian asceticism of the greatest of these bishops, however, that appealed most strongly to the people; and a number of the fourth-, fifth- and sixth-century monastic bishops were recognized as saints, with churches dedicated to them in the city and a lively celebration of their feast days. This was true of Justus who had left his position as bishop in order to live the life of a monk in Egypt, the birthplace of monasticism. After his death, his relics were returned to Lyon and were the subject of veneration. Eucherius was a married man when he felt the call to a monastic life, and both he and his wife joined monasteries. Like St Cuthbert he retired even further from the island monastery of Lerins to a more remote isle, where he gained a great reputation for holiness. Again like St Cuthbert, he was called to be bishop directly because of his standing among the people as a holy ascetic.

WILFRID TONSURED AS A MONK

The lives of holy martyrs and ascetics would have been recalled daily in Lyon in the churches dedicated to them. The ordinary Christian would have been familiar with the details of their lives. They must have been a continuing inspiration to any bishop who took his faith seriously. Wilfrid lived for over three years with the Bishop of Lyon and would have attended the celebrations of the saints' days and gained a profound knowledge of liturgical celebration. His practical experience was enhanced by daily study with tutors, and his love for the monastic life deepened.

If Wilfrid received his secondary education in Lindisfarne and Rome, his university was Lyon with its 600 years of vigorous and continuous Christian tradition. At the end of his three years he graduated, receiving the monastic tonsure from his father in God, Bishop Annemund.

THE YOUNG CONFESSOR

Wilfrid's most momentous experience in Lyon was to be his last there. In 657 the Merovingian (Frankish) king had died, leaving a seven-year-old as his heir. This boy was Annemund's godson. Those dukes who expected to gain power during the minority of the successor to the throne apparently feared the bishop. Annemund was suddenly seized, tried and executed. His young 'son' Wilfrid, despite the bishop's prohibition, insisted on accompanying him in the hope that he too would receive the crown of martyrdom. 'What better', he said, 'than that father and son die at once and go to Christ together.'

Seeing him stripped and ready for death, the judges asked who he was. On learning that he was an Englishman from overseas, they spared him. Denied the crown of early martyrdom, Wilfrid had shown himself a worthy 'confessor' of Christ. He was to receive his crown only after a long and arduous journey.

Notes

1   Both Bede and Eddius refer to the bishop as Dalfinus, but scholars are agreed that Dalfinus was the secular ruler and the brother of Annemund.
2   The Monophysites are those who talk of Christ having one nature, or *physis*, as opposed to the Orthodox view that Christ is one person in two natures, divine and human.
3   The heresy of Monothelitism attempted to reconcile the differences between the Orthodox and Monophysites by saying that Christ had only one will.
4   The account of these martyrs is to be found in Eusebius, *Ecclesiastical History* Book V, tr. H. J. Lawlor and J. E. L. Oulton (SPCK, 1927, pages 139–49).

Part III

Abbot, Priest and Bishop

8

Abbot of Ripon (660)

KING ALCHFRID

On returning to Britain, Bede tells us that Wilfrid 'made friends with King Alchfrid'. Eddius puts it more colourfully: 'Their souls intertwined in the most wonderful way, just as we read of David's soul being knit to Jonathan's.' Alchfrid was Oswy's son and had been made sub-king of Deira to succeed Ethelwald, who was killed fighting against his own people. This friendship was very important to Wilfrid on his return to Northumbria after so many years abroad.

Alchfrid followed the church traditions of Queen Eanfled and not the Irish customs of Oswy. He was delighted to find an eloquent monk, deeply versed in the traditions of Gaul and Rome, and made Wilfrid his instructor in the faith. He gave him 30 hides of land at Ripon, which was enough to support 30 families. This land had been given to monks in the Irish tradition, including the English Cuthbert and Eata, but was now taken from them, as they were not prepared to adopt 'catholic' ways. Wilfrid was made abbot of the new community. So he began his work in his own homeland by establishing the practices he had learned in Rome and Lyon, with the full support of the king.

In Ripon Wilfrid built one of his great churches. But it was the monastery that was at the heart of his life. His cell at Ripon remained his true home throughout his many years of exile. And it was in Ripon that he was buried nearly 50 years later.

WILFRID ORDAINED PRIEST

In 664 an interesting visitor arrived at Ripon. His name was Agilbert. He was a Frank who had become a bishop in Gaul and had then gone to Ireland to study the Scriptures. From Ireland he went as bishop to the kingdom of the West Saxons. But the king there grew tired of his Frankish accent, his 'barbarous speech', and divided his see. Agilbert returned to Gaul and accepted the bishopric of Paris, which he held from some time after 664 until his death. His life is an illustration of the rich diversity of Christian influence on Britain – Irish, Gallic, Frankish and Roman.

At the request of King Alchfrid, Agilbert ordained Wilfrid to the priesthood in his own monastery of Ripon. It was Agilbert who brought Wilfrid to the fore at the meeting often called the synod of Whitby.

9

The Advocate at Whitby

King Oswy called the meeting at Whitby and he presided over it. It was not unusual for kings to be involved in the summoning of councils of the Church. The emperor Constantine had called the Council of Nicaea to resolve a question of heresy, which was causing division in his empire. Oswy was acting in a similar way, to resolve a matter of church practice that was a source of division in his kingdom.

The purpose of the synod of Whitby was to resolve the question of the date of Easter. It was important that the unity of the Church should be particularly clear on the most important festival of the year. As it was, those who followed the 'Irish' calendar – and they included Oswy himself and the monastics of Lindisfarne and Whitby – could be celebrating the resurrection while those who followed the 'Roman' date, Queen Eanfled and King Alchfrid included, were still keeping the fast of Lent. This was bad for the unity of the Church, but it could also cause political disunity in Northumbria. Oswy summoned both political and religious leaders to Whitby.

The choice of the abbey at Whitby is interesting. It was only a decade old, but had become one of the most important monasteries in the whole country. It had been founded by a remarkable woman, St Hilda.

St Hilda

Of royal birth, Hilda was baptized at the age of 13 by Paulinus, Queen Ethelberga's bishop, and was 20 years old in 634 when King Oswald brought Aidan to Northumbria. At the age of 33, Hilda went to the house of relatives in East Anglia, planning to join her sister as a nun in Gaul. The monasteries of Gaul had a rich history, dating back to the beginnings of Christian monasticism and deriving directly from the Egyptian desert. Chelles, where Hilda's sister was 'living as a stranger for the Lord's sake', exerted a great pull on those in Britain with a monastic calling, and Hilda's wish to follow her sister was not unusual. But Aidan did not want to lose such a gem, and he called her to found her own monastery in Deira. She established a monastic house at Hartlepool in the same year that the teenage Wilfrid entered Lindisfarne. She created a second monastery at Tadcaster and finally she founded the double monastery at Whitby.

Double monasteries were those with separate accommodation for men and women, who shared much of the monastic life and work. Common among the Franks and Anglo-Saxons, they always had an abbess in charge. The monastery of St Milburga in Wenlock, the 'holy place' of Mercia, and that of her sister St Mildred in Thanet, are other examples.

All who knew Hilda called her 'mother', 'because of her outstanding devotion and grace'. She established a clear rule, designed to inculcate the virtues of peace and charity, and there was a strong emphasis on biblical study and the practice of good works. Many sought guidance from her; ordinary people, princes and kings. Her monastery produced no fewer than five bishops as well as Caedmon, the first poet of the Anglo-Saxon tongue. Chief among her guides was Aidan, and the monastery followed the Irish traditions that became the focus of attention at the famous synod of 664.

THE SYNOD OF WHITBY (664)

Both kings were present: the father, Oswy, fluent in the Irish language and nurtured in the Irish tradition; the son, Alchfrid, instructed by Wilfrid and dedicated to the ways of the continental church. Queen Eanfled's priest, Romanus, and the deacon James, a courageous survivor of the original Kentish mission of Paulinus, were on the Roman side. So was the senior churchman present, Bishop Agilbert. Abbess Hilda and all her monastics, followers of the beloved St Aidan, supported the Irish position, as did the venerable St Cedd, who acted as 'most careful interpreter' for this multilingual gathering.

King Oswy presided and ordered Agilbert to present the tradition he followed. However, Agilbert requested the king to allow Wilfrid to speak on his behalf, as he would be able to expound things more clearly in the English language than he could through an interpreter.

But it was certainly more than a simple question of Agilbert's Frankish tongue that led to the choice of Wilfrid, one of the youngest people present in this most august gathering. His keen mind and handsome bearing had impressed Queen Eanfled when first she met him, when he was 14. Since then he had been schooled in Lindisfarne, Canterbury, Lyon and Rome and had four years' experience of leadership as Abbot of Ripon. His time at Lindisfarne would have given him a thorough knowledge of Irish customs, and his years in Gaul and Rome a deep understanding of the traditions of the wider Church.

This was Wilfrid's first appearance on the public stage. His words lucid, his theology clear and his sense of ecclesiastical order assured, he was an eloquent champion of the continental tradition.

Bede leaves us with an indelible impression of this occasion. Like contestants in the arena, Colman – Bishop and Abbot of Lindisfarne, and defender of ancient Irish custom and the practices of Holy Columba of Iona – and Wilfrid of Ripon confronted one another before the noblest and most learned in the kingdom.

Colman's case was strong: the Irish dating of Easter had the authority of the apostle and evangelist John, and it was ever the practice of St Columba and the holy fathers of Iona. Many of those present would have been moved by the power of his argument. Did they in Northumbria not owe their faith to Irish Aidan, whose gentle holiness was evident to all?

But Wilfrid marshalled his arguments with clarity and drove them home with remorseless rhetorical power. How could the Irish – supported only by Picts and Britons, their obstinate accomplices – living on these remote islands, foolishly set themselves up against the rest of the Christian world in Africa, Asia, Egypt, Greece and Rome where the apostles Peter and Paul lived, taught, suffered and were buried? Colman's expostulation about the use of the word 'foolish' gave Wilfrid the opening to expound the calendar and the history of the celebration of Easter with lucidity and unanswerable logic.

He accepted that the apostle John had kept the 'Law of Moses' and celebrated Pascha on the fourteenth of the month, on whatever day of the week that fell. This was because the apostles 'were not able immediately to abrogate the observances of the Law once given by God, lest they give offence to believers who were Jews'. As the gospel spread through the world, this ceased to be necessary, and St Peter, recalling that Christ rose on the day after the Sabbath, waited for the first occurrence of the 'morrow of the Sabbath' following the fourteenth and celebrated on that day. He did not deny the sanctity of Columba, nor did he think that the Ionan way of keeping Easter was 'seriously harmful', so long as they were unaware of the catholic reckoning. But Colman did know and would certainly be committing a sin in failing to conform to the Apostolic See and the universal Church. In addition to these historical arguments concerning the apostolic tradition, there was also a detailed debate about the cycles for the calculation of the lunar and solar calendars, demonstrating that both men had a good technical knowledge of these complex issues.

King Oswy listened carefully to the arguments on both sides. In the end he smiled and asked, 'Tell me, which is greater in the kingdom of Heaven, Columba or the apostle Peter?' The decision had been made and from that day Northumbria adopted the 'Roman' date of Easter.

Some time after the meeting we learn that Alchfrid attacked his father. We do not know how, why or when this took place. It has been suggested that the issue of the date of Easter played a part in this conflict; the son Alchfrid marshalling support behind the banner of the orthodox date against the insular Easter of his father. This, argues Mayr Harting,[1] would account for Oswy's smile as he came down on the side of St Peter and took the wind out of Alchfrid's sails. Some time after 664 Alchfrid disappeared from the scene. Doubtless he met an unnatural end.

Many of those who conformed to the orthodox date kept their close links with Ireland and Irish traditions of learning. This was true of Hilda and the monastery of Whitby, as it was of her disciple Bosa, who replaced Wilfrid as bishop of York when he was exiled in 678. Others of this outlook such as Cedd and Eata were to become bishops, as was that 'gentle and attractive teacher' Egfrid, who lived much of his life as a monk in Leinster. He was the driving force behind the Frisian mission of Willibrord and finally won over the monks of Iona on the Easter question.

10

The Bishop (664–678)

Wilfrid was chosen to be bishop in 664. It was a fateful year. Following the synod of Whitby, the respected Bishop Colman left Lindisfarne for Inishbofin. His successor, Tuda, died soon after his appointment in an outbreak of the plague, as did a number of other bishops, including the Archbishop of Canterbury. It became almost impossible to get three bishops together to consecrate a new one. The problems were exacerbated by the conflict between King Alchfrid and his father Oswy, which culminated in Alchfrid's disappearance. Was the eclipse of the sun that happened on 3 May a symbol of this dark and murky time?

Both kings wanted Wilfrid to be consecrated in Gaul and provided generously for his journey. The consecration in Gaul of a bishop for the north of Britain would have given an emphatic statement to the world about the catholicity of the Northumbrian church and demonstrate that it was part of the continental mainstream. It appealed to Wilfrid, particularly as Agilbert, who had ordained him priest, was to be involved. Consecrations on the continent were not unusual and there was, in any case, the difficulty of finding three bishops in Britain.

CONSECRATION IN GAUL

The consecration was a grand affair. It was important to the Anglian kings that their bishop arrive in state, and they had provided him with 'a vast sum of money'. The service of consecration was in keeping with the majesty of the occasion of the creation of a new bishop for a foreign land. Gallic liturgical tradition was noted for its grandeur and rich elaboration and, as part of the ceremony, Wilfrid was borne aloft on a golden throne, carried on the shoulders of 12 bishops as the choirs sang their canticles and songs. Unaccountably, Wilfrid was delayed in Gaul, and he was to return to a Northumbria in which there had been radical changes.

WILD MEN OF SUSSEX

On the voyage home from Gaul, Wilfrid and his people were singing the psalms when a sudden, violent storm with a howling south-east wind drove their boat onto the coast of the South Saxons and left them stranded high on the shore. They were immediately set upon by a horde of pagans intent on looting and taking slaves. Wilfrid's soothing words and promise of money only elicited the retort that anything washed up on their shore was theirs. Their chief priest stood on a mound and invoked curses on them as his people prepared to attack, but he was struck down by a stone flung from a sling by one of Wilfrid's companions. Three times the pagans hurled themselves on the Christians. Wilfrid and his priests fell on their knees and prayed for God's help and his men, well-armed and committed, drove back the attackers with loss of life on both sides.

Finally the Saxon king himself appeared and his people prepared for a massive onslaught. Wilfrid prayed again and the tide came sweeping up the shore so that they could cast off and make for the deep. The wind had swung round to the south-west and they were carried safely to Sandwich. Wilfrid's next visit to the land of the South Saxons was to be longer and more fruitful.

YORK USURPED

He arrived home to find Alchfrid no more; Oswy the sole king of Northumbria; and Chad, Bishop of York. Alchfrid had proposed Wilfrid for bishop, but it was with 'the advice and consent' of his father Oswy that Wilfrid was sent to Gaul and it was while he was abroad that Oswy had Chad made Bishop of York, which lay in Alchfrid's kingdom of Deira.

What had happened to Alchfrid? Did Oswy, anticipating or planning conflict with his son, want Wilfrid out of the way, or was the delay in Gaul due to Alchfrid's unsuccessful 'rebellion' and Wilfrid's uncertainty about the reception he would receive from Oswy? We can only speculate on these things as our sources tell us nothing about the conflict between Oswy and Alchfrid other than that it took place. Whatever happened, Wilfrid's first years as bishop followed considerable political turmoil, which included the appointment of another bishop in his place.

There is one interpretation of these events according to which Tuda of Lindisfarne was appointed to Bernicia and Wilfrid to Deira. On Tuda's death during Wilfrid's absence, Chad was appointed Bishop of Northumbria with his centre at York, to break with the Irish traditions of Lindisfarne. When Wilfrid came back to take up his position in Deira, he worked quietly from Ripon. This interpretation is difficult to sustain as there is no hint in our sources of such a division of the diocese at this time.

It is more likely that when he returned from Gaul and found that the saintly Chad was bishop of York, Wilfrid decided to withdraw to Ripon to take up his former life as abbot. He must have had complex feelings. There was his love of the monastic life and of his monastery at Ripon, but also the sense of his new vocation and mission as bishop. The political realities were obvious: his friend and protector, Alchfrid, had gone; the appointment of Chad had been at Oswy's behest; and the see of Canterbury, to which appeal could be made, was vacant.

THE PERIPATETIC BISHOP (665–668)

Canterbury was not the only vacant see, Mercia too was without a bishop and Wilfrid was called upon to act as bishop in both kingdoms. Wulfhere, King of Mercia, had a great liking for him, called upon him frequently and gave him many gifts of land, which Wilfrid used to found monasteries. He was to spend more than ten years of his old age in Mercia and was to die in one of his Mercian monasteries. In Kent he ordained many priests and deacons at the behest of King Egbert.

So, for three years, Wilfrid took a leading part in building up the church throughout the Midlands and south-east of Britain after the depredations of the plague, which had left dioceses without bishops and parishes without priests. In 668 the new archbishop arrived. He deposed Chad, installed Wilfrid at York and relieved him of his responsibilities in the south. Another giant of the seventh century had come to Britain – St Theodore.

Born in Tarsus at the beginning of the century, educated at Antioch and Constantinople, the Greek Theodore had, like many of the Christians of Syria, taken refuge in Rome from the Persian and Arab invasions of the East. There he had lived for many years as a simple monk. But like others of his fellow Greeks in Rome, he had a deep understanding of Orthodox theology and of the threat of the heresy of Monothelitism then being imposed by the Byzantine emperors. He was probably present – a certain 'monk Theodore' is mentioned among those attending – at the council in Rome at the Lateran that condemned the heresy and led to the persecution of Pope Martin. He would have known Maximus the Confessor and his great theological writings. At the age of 66 he was called by the Bishop of Rome to become Archbishop of Canterbury.

On the death of Deusdedit, the Archbishop of Canterbury, in 664, King Oswy had consulted King Egbert of Kent and selected a certain Wigheard as a possible successor and sent him to Rome for consecration. But the plague accompanied him and he died soon after his arrival. The Pope describes this and the decisions he then made in a letter to the English kings. His choice of an old Syrian-Greek monk seems extraordinary, but it was an inspired choice.

Theodore is possibly the greatest bishop ever to have held the see of Canterbury. In his 21 years as archbishop, he created a diocesan structure so well-tuned to the diverse cultural and geographical realities of the country that many of the dioceses he created remain in place to this day. He founded a school at Canterbury at which he himself taught and that became the greatest centre of learning in western Christendom. The first to act as primate of all England, he held councils of the whole church to establish an ordered and common pattern of life in all the disparate kingdoms of the land. He wrote a book that was to act as a guide to spiritual and moral life for centuries to come.

But for all his love of canonical order, Theodore was prepared to temper the rigours of canon law to the complexities of the world. An orthodox bishop can subordinate legal punctiliousness to the demands of the overriding 'law' of love and, as a shrewd and sensitive judge of character with a sound understanding of the political realities of his day, he was able to do so pragmatically and to good effect. It is an area where judgements can differ and it was precisely here that he and Wilfrid were later to come into conflict.

WILFRID, BISHOP OF YORK (669–678)

Theodore's first act, however, was to apply the canons to the situation in York; Chad was deposed and Wilfrid installed as rightful bishop in 669. Whatever the politics behind the appointment of Chad, Oswy was now close to his new bishop, so much so that he persuaded Wilfrid to accompany him to Rome so that 'he could end his life among its holy places'. His wish was not fulfilled as he died of illness early in 670, and his probably illegitimate son Egfrid succeeded him. A man learned in the Irish tradition and a successful warrior, Egfrid enlarged his kingdom by inflicting defeats on the Picts to the north and the Mercians to the south, thus considerably enlarging Wilfrid's diocese.

Wilfrid had now had three years' experience as bishop in two other kingdoms and time to pray and reflect in his monastery at Ripon. His priorities clear, he immediately set to work with great energy and for the next nine years he applied all that he had learnt in Lyon and Rome about the duties of a bishop.

There was the pastoral and administrative work of the enormous diocese to be carried out and the evidence is that this was done effectively. But such regular, daily responsibilities are unremarkable and our sources tell us about his more exceptional and visible work. First there was the great church at York, founded by Paulinus. This was in a sorry state, with water streaming through the rotten roof, the walls decaying and filthy with the mess of nesting birds. Wilfrid employed good craftsmen to replace the timbers and to cover the whole roof with lead. The walls were scrubbed and the windows glazed so that the birds were kept out, but the light allowed in. He also took practical steps to ensure a steady income stream for the continued maintenance of this great building, by acquiring land and endowments for the church.

Wilfrid's next building project was a new church at Ripon, dedicated to St Peter. This was followed by another, dedicated to St Andrew, at Hexham. The dedications reflect his devotion to the apostles at whose tombs he had prayed on his pilgrimage to Rome. They were grand buildings of dressed stone, with side aisles, decorated columns, crypts and staircases. Their like, says Eddius, had not before been seen north of the Alps. The altars were well provided with vessels, the clergy with vestments, and the inside of the buildings were beautifully decorated. We are left no detailed description of the iconography, but we know that Wilfrid always brought back many relics and rich objects from his visits abroad. On one of his visits to Rome, Eddius tells us that he amassed an enormous number of things for the beautification of the churches, but says it would be 'tedious' to enumerate them. They would, of course, be well known to Eddius' immediate audience, the monks of Wilfrid's monasteries who saw them every day.

A frustrated posterity can gain an idea of the inside of Wilfrid's churches by turning to the detailed account of the iconography of the monasteries of St Peter at Wearmouth and St Paul at Jarrow, provided by Bede in his history of the abbots. The icons came from the Mediterranean world as a result of the tireless travelling and collecting of the monastery's founder, Benedict Biscop, and his companions, including Ceolfrid, the first Abbot of Jarrow, who was ordained to the priesthood by Wilfrid. Scenes from the life of Christ were depicted, and there were large icons of the Lord Himself and of the Holy Mother of God; pictures of the 12 apostles were arranged to reach from wall to wall on the central arch. In the monastery at Jarrow there was a complete sequence of biblical events carefully arranged to show the fulfilment of the Old Testament in the New; Isaac carrying the wood on which he was to be burnt as a sacrifice was immediately below the icon of Christ carrying his cross; and the serpent lifted up by Moses in the desert was shown to foreshadow the lifting up of Christ on the cross.

The Gospels use Old Testament events as 'types', fulfilled in the life of Christ, and this 'typology' was characteristic of the hymns of the great feasts and the writings of the fathers. Icons, words, music and the drama of processions and entrances were a liturgical whole for the glorification of God and the instruction of his people. Such theologically ordered iconography remained normal in eastern Christendom but, in the seventh century, when iconoclasm was at its height in the East, the churches of Northumbria gave as full an expression of the wholeness of Christian liturgical life as anywhere.

ILLUMINATED MANUSCRIPTS AND RICH WORSHIP

This wholeness is equally true of the illuminated manuscipts. These drew on all the traditions then alive in Northumbria; the sinuous forms and jaunty mouths of Anglo-Saxon animals join ancient Irish spirals, the geometric forms of Roman pavement mosaics and the iconographic perceptions of Byzantine Italy in a breathtaking synthesis. Revered as a proclamation of God's final and saving self-revelation, the illuminated copies of the Gospels are the fulfilment of all that is best in earlier artistic insights. The Lindisfarne Gospels; the great Bible that Abbot Ceolfrid gave to the Bishop of Rome, still preserved in Florence, and the many other illuminated works destroyed in the Viking invasions were expressions of this rich understanding of the Christian faith.

The manuscripts produced by the scriptorium at Ripon have not been preserved, but we know that this important part of the preaching of the gospel also formed part of Wilfrid's evangelical work. The church at Ripon was adorned as 'the bridal-chamber of the true Bridegroom and Bride with gold and silver and every shade of purple', and the altar was vested in purple woven with gold. Royal gold and imperial purple, were used to glorify the King of all kings. In such a place, the living word of God – the book of the Gospels – was an equally glorious creation, written in letters of pure gold on 'parchment all empurpled and illuminated'.

The fulness of worship was completed by attention to the reading, chanting and singing. Wilfrid himself would have been fluent in the established musical tones, and he brought experienced cantors to teach his people both the musical tradition and the rich patterns of liturgical order. He insisted on full antiphonal singing, the practice established in the churches of the continent. The voices of the two choirs – of the cantors, and of the priests and deacons – each with its own character, would have had a texture as rich and full as the icons and manuscripts. It was another expression of the wholeness of the gospel.

A NEW ENEMY

These years of vigorous, unfettered episcopal activity for Wilfrid were to be suddenly cut short. An enemy appeared, Egfrid's new queen. His first queen was Etheldreda, also known as St Audrey, who was to become Abbess of Ely. Daughter of the devout, Christian King Anna of the East Angles, she had been briefly married to a prince of the South Gyrwas in the Fens, who died soon after the marriage. She was then given to the 15-year-old Egfrid. That marriage lasted 12 years, but was never consummated as she had decided to live a life of perpetual virginity. Knowing that she held Wilfrid 'in high regard', Egfrid promised to give him great estates and wealth if he would persuade her to change her mind. In the end, Wilfrid persuaded the king to allow her to 'serve Christ the only true King in a convent'. It was Wilfrid who clothed her as a nun.

Egfrid's new queen, Irminburga, is not mentioned by Bede; she did not conform to his requirements of providing examples of 'good deeds' to encourage his readers. Eddius compares her to Jezebel. He says that she stirred up the king to envy by listing all Wilfrid's possessions, the majesty of his buildings and the number and magnificence of his followers. Her animosity might have had a more particular source. Wilfrid's great church at Hexham was built on land given to him by Queen Etheldreda and, together with Ripon, it was his most precious jewel. It is possible to understand how the new queen wanted to sweep away all memory of her pious predecessor, and of the monk who acted as her adviser and whose eloquence had such influence over her husband.

Irminburga had a powerful personality and Egfrid was persuaded. Wilfrid was driven out of Northumbria.

Note

1 H. Mayr-Harting, *The Coming of Christianity to Anglo-Saxon England*. Batsford, 1972.

Part IV

Exile

11

A Dangerous Journey

As we have seen, there was a serious shortage of bishops on Theodore's arrival in Britain. Not only did Theodore set about filling the vacancies, but also he created a number of new dioceses, as mentioned already. He established the see of Worcester to serve the people of the Severn valley, and the see of Hereford for the tribe that lived in that area. A separate diocese was established for the kingdom of Lindsey. What was to be done about the enormous kingdom of Northumbria?

Northumbria was formed from the often uneasy unification of Bernicia in the north and Deira in the south, with borders that extended north to Pictland. The province of Lindsey had been part of Northumbria when it was in the ascendancy over Mercia. Before Theodore's arrival, one bishop had served the whole kingdom, however far it extended. Wilfrid, according to Bede, ruled as bishop 'all the lands of the Northumbrians and Picts to the borders of Oswy's realms'.

This had a certain political logic. But it ignored the historical distinction between Deira and Bernicia, the separate history of Lindsey and the completely distinct Pictish lands. It also demanded exceptional administrative abilities and physical prowess of the bishop. Wilfrid doubtless had these qualities, but the church could not be organized on the assumption that all bishops were so endowed. Northumbria needed to be divided and Wilfrid's expulsion by the king gave an opportunity for this to be done.

True to his principles of creating small dioceses that corresponded to natural boundaries, Theodore established new sees based on Hexham and Lindisfarne in Bernicia, on Ripon and

59

York in Deira, and consecrated the Irish-educated Trumwine to serve the newly acquired Pictish territories.

As we have noted, Wilfrid was expelled from his see by King Egfrid. It was done for personal reasons, without reference to church law, and had no moral or theological grounds. There was no basis for an appeal to an ecclesiastical authority against the blatant exercise of political power. But once Theodore had divided his diocese and appointed three new bishops, there was a case to be made for a breach of church law. Theodore had not deposed Wilfrid, but he had acquiesced in his deposition. He had acted promptly to ensure that the people of Northumbria had the necessary episcopal oversight for their needs. Had he gone through a correct procedure for deposing the bishop, giving grounds and sustaining a case against him, then he would have acted in a canonically sound manner. The fact that he did not do so is good reason for believing that there were no such grounds.

Theodore had a meeting with King Egfrid and his queen, who explained their intentions to him and told him of their determination to humiliate Wilfrid. According to Eddius, Theodore's acquiescence was ensured by bribes, 'for money will blind even the wisest'. There is no reason to believe this charge, which is one of the more striking examples of Eddius' inability to deal fairly with his hero's opponents. It is completely out of character with all that we know of Theodore. Much more likely is that he understood the implacable hatred of Queen Irminburga for Wilfrid and the impossiblity of effecting any change, and acted in what he considered the best interests of the church.

In the case of a dispute involving a bishop, appeal would normally be made to other local bishops, or to the provincial bishop. In a dispute involving a provincial bishop, appeal would be made to the patriarch. It was therefore natural for Wilfrid to take his dispute to the Bishop of Rome. This was the cause of the second of Wilfrid's three journeys to Rome.

ATTEMPTS ON WILFRID'S LIFE

So fierce was the enmity towards Wilfrid that several attempts were made on his life. Knowing that he was journeying to Rome, his enemies sent to the King of the Franks and a certain Duke

Ebroin and asked them to exile him for good or to kill all his companions and steal his goods as he journeyed through their lands. On his previous crossing of the channel, Wilfrid had been driven by an east wind onto the shores of the South Saxons. On this occasion a gentle west wind blew him out of danger to Frisia. The pagans of Sussex had met him with armed force; the pagans of Frisia, under their King Aldgisl, welcomed him with warm hospitality.

Meanwhile Ebroin's thugs had found an English bishop travelling to Rome to appeal to the Pope about his deposition by Theodore from the see of Lichfield. His name was Winfrid. Small wonder that he was mistaken for Wilfrid. He was beaten, robbed and left naked, and some of his followers were killed.

Having discovered his mistake, Ebroin then tried to bribe King Aldgisl. He offered him a bushel of gold to send Wilfrid to him alive or, failing that, to slay him and send his head. King Aldgisl was entertaining Wilfrid and his companions and all his own people to a feast, and had the letter read aloud before them. He then took it, tore it up and threw the pieces onto the blazing fire. 'Tell your lord,' he said to Ebroin's messengers, 'what you now hear me say: Thus may the Creator of all things rend and destroy the life and lands of him who perjures himself before God and breaks the pact he has made. Even thus may he be torn to pieces and burn to ashes.'

THE APOSTLE TO FRISIA (678–679)

Wilfrid stayed the winter and, with the king's permission, daily preached the saving truths of the gospel. All but a few of the chiefs and thousands of the common people were baptized. On the foundation laid by Wilfrid, Willibrord, one of his own Ripon monks, was to build, earning the title of 'apostle of the Frisians'.

Leaving Frisia, Wilfrid journeyed through the Frankish kingdom of Dagobert II, who was well known to him. Dagobert had been exiled in his youth, and had taken refuge in Ireland for many years. When his friends discovered that he was still alive they contacted Wilfrid, presumably knowing him from his time in Gaul, to see if he could help Dagobert to return. This Wilfrid did. He arranged for him to come to Northumbria and then equipped him with arms and men so that he was able to return and take up his throne. He was king for only three years and, as we shall see, was not there to welcome Wilfrid on his return journey.

Now in a position to make gifts to Wilfrid in gratitude for his former friendship, Dagobert welcomed him warmly and offered him the chief bishopric of his realm, Strasbourg. On Wilfrid's refusal, he showered him with gifts and gave him one of his bishops to act as his guide as far as Lombardy in north Italy.

Here, once again, Wilfrid's enemies had preceded him and had attempted to bribe the Lombard king to lay hands on him and prevent his reaching Rome. He, like Dagobert and so many other Germanic kings, had spent years in exile and had a natural sympathy with the exiled Angle. His own protector in exile had been a pagan 'King of the Huns', who had acted honourably when approached with bribes by his enemies. How much more should he 'who knows the true God, refuse to send my soul to perdition'. Wilfrid, pursued by his enemies across the continent, finally arrived safely in Rome.

12

Wilfrid's Second Visit to Rome

Wilfrid's appeal against Archbishop Theodore's division of his diocese was made to the Roman synod under the Sicilian Pope Agatho, who had already been involved in British affairs and had sent John, the chief cantor of St Peter's, with Benedict Biscop to teach the Roman way of chanting to the church in Northumbria. John, who was an abbot, also had another duty to perform while in Britain, which was to collect a written statement of the faith in answer to the Monothelite heresy. A great council of the Church was being assembled at Constantinople, later to be recognized as the Sixth Ecumenical Council, to deal with this heresy, and the Pope was collecting statements from all the churches in the West to forward to Constantinople. Theodore called a council of the whole church in Britain at Hatfield, on the borders of Deira and Lindsey, to agree a common statement. Similar councils were being held in Gaul and elsewhere. Archbishop Theodore was in fact an expert on this issue and the Pope had asked him to attend the Roman council that dealt with it. He declined on the grounds of age and his enormous commitments.

THE APPEAL TO THE ROMAN SYNOD (679)

It was at this very time, when momentous councils of the Church were being held, that Wilfrid arrived in Rome to make his appeal. Neither Bede nor Eddius records the letters of Archbishop Theodore that were already in the Pope's hands on Wilfrid's arrival, but we have the text of Wilfrid's petition, which forms Chapter 30 of Eddius' *Life*.

Wilfrid said that he could not understand how so venerable a man as Theodore Archbishop of Canterbury could bring himself to consecrate three bishops to replace him in the see of York, without reference to him. Following this he had taken care to cause no strife or dissension, but had simply withdrawn and set about appealing in the correct canonical manner and informed his fellow bishops of the matter. He had committed no crime, but should the synod decide that he was to be considered deposed, he would accept the decision 'with humble devotion'. If restored, he asked that the usurping bishops be deposed and that, if it seemed good to the archbishop and the other bishops to divide the diocese of Northumbria, new bishops be chosen from the local people, rather than from among strangers and outsiders.

There are two striking things about this petition. The first is Wilfrid's readiness to obey the decisions of Rome, even if this should mean losing his see. The second is that he was prepared to accept the division of his diocese if this was considered the best solution. There is no evidence here of an arrogant bishop keen on disputes. He was simply determined that the canons of the Church should not be flouted at the demand of the king.

The synod's decision went in Wilfrid's favour. He was to be fully restored and the three new bishops deposed. It appears that this was decided on the basis of the canons, without reference to local conditions. It is odd that the opportunity was not taken to approve the division of the diocese and to reach a long-term solution with which Theodore and the other bishops would have been happy. Agatho's approach was very different from that of his successor John, who was to hear a similar appeal from Wilfrid 30 years later and examined the whole situation in great detail over several months. Perhaps this was because of the other pressures on Agatho, for whom the most urgent priority was the work of preparing a council on Monothelitism so that the thoughts of the western churches could be forwarded to Constantinople.

In fact this council was held immediately after the hearing of Wilfrid's case, and Wilfrid, now exonerated from all charges, was asked to sit at the council of 125 bishops and to speak 'on behalf of all the northern part of Britain and Ireland and the islands inhabited by Angles, Britons, Picts and Scots'. Although he was in dispute with Theodore over the order of the church, the two were completely at one on doctrine. The range of lands on whose behalf Wilfrid was asked to speak is remarkable. The extent of Northumbria and therefore of the jurisdiction of its one bishop was enormous and this explains most of the list. Wilfrid's detailed knowledge of the teaching of Iona, with its profound and continuing links with Northumbria, was obviously known in Rome. This would explain how he came to be asked to speak on behalf of the Scots who inhabited the islands. That he was asked to speak on behalf of the north of Ireland is more extraordinary, but given their intimacy with Iona, was not unreasonable. His appearance at this synod was to stand him in good stead when, in his old age, he was next to appear before the Pope in synod.

Wilfrid's love for Rome, with its churches containing the relics of the martyred apostles, made it difficult for him to leave. The appeal over, he was content to pray at these holy sites as a pilgrim, just as he had been as a young man a quarter of a century before. Eventually the Pope directed him to return. Knowing the needs of the churches in Britain, he made a great collection from the riches of Rome – carefully labelled relics, cloths and other items to beautify the liturgy and the house of God – to take back with him to Northumbria.

A NEW THREAT TO WILFRID'S LIFE

Pursued on the outward journey by his enemies, Wilfrid very nearly failed to return because of the enemies of his friend Dagobert. Not long after Wilfrid left him on his way to Rome, Dagobert was assassinated. Not knowing of Dagobert's fate, Wilfrid reached the land of the Franks to be met by an army, at the head of which was a bishop. This bishop upbraided Wilfrid for his boldness in coming there, as he deserved to be put to death for 'making Dagobert king'.

Association with kings could be advantageous, but also dangerous. The last time Wilfrid was met by military force, in Sussex, his appeals for peace had been rejected and his companions were forced to fight. On this occasion he was confronted by a well-prepared army that had come out to kill him, not by an armed band that chanced upon his party. If he were forced into fighting in self-defence, he had no chance of success. All depended on his powers of persuasion.

The Frankish bishop gave the reasons for Dagobert's death: he had spurned the advice of the elders; he had laid waste their cities;

he had imposed a humiliating tribute on his people and despised the Church of God. All this was laid at the door of Wilfrid.

Wilfrid's reply was:

> In the name of Jesus Christ what I say is true; by the holy apostle Peter I swear I do not lie. It was in accordance with God's command to the people of Israel when they dwelt as strangers in a foreign land that I helped and cherished King Dagobert, then an exile and wanderer. I raised him up not to your harm but for your good, sending him to build up your cities, to put spirit into your citizens, to counsel your senate, and, as he promised in the Lord's name, to defend the Church. Most righteous bishop, if an exile in my own country, and one of royal blood, had come to your lordship, where else would your duty have lain?

The appeal to the deep-seated sense of honour common to traditional communities, whether Celtic, Germanic or Roman, was very powerful. Linking it to the divine commandments of the Bible was overwhelming, and humbled the bellicose bishop. 'The Lord preserve your goings out and your comings in,' he said. 'Pardon me, for, like the patriarch Judah, I see that you are more righteous than I. The Lord be with you, and may the apostle Peter be your aid.'

KING EGFRID THROWS WILFRID INTO GAOL (680)

Wilfrid had escaped from many dangers since leaving Britain, and he was returning with the support of the Holy See for his complete restoration. On his arrival in Northumbria he was treated with ignominy. All the principal clergy and people were called together to hear the papal decision. It was totally rejected, some even alleging that it had been obtained by bribery. The king, in council, and with the consent of the local bishops, condemned Wilfrid to nine months in gaol. He was to have all but his clothes taken from him and to be put in solitary confinement. His followers were to be scattered and no friend allowed near him. Most shocking of all, the queen seized the precious relics that Wilfrid had so lovingly collected, and strung them together into a necklace, which she wore ostentatiously.

Before being taken to his cell, Wilfrid was allowed to talk to his people. With calm assurance he laid before them the experience of all those in the Bible who were loved by God. Beginning with the patriarchs of the Old Testament and recalling the lives of Moses, Aaron and all the prophets, he reminded them that they all had endured persecution. But their trust was not in human beings but in God. 'The Great Shepherd of the Sheep and Head of the Whole Church, Jesus Christ, was crucified by the Jews and His disciples scattered.' Later they were dispersed through the whole world and received the crowns of martyrdom. They were sustained by the words of the Epistle to the Hebrews: 'My son, neglect not the discipline of the Lord; neither be thou wearied whilst thou art rebuked by him. For whom the Lord loveth he chastiseth.'

This moving address to his friends was made the more powerful by Wilfrid's composure in the face of suffering. But ultimately its strength lay in his sense of the vital presence of the Lord and his profound love for the Scriptures, the living word of God, the recalling of which came as easily to him as the beating of his heart. His final words of encouragement were also taken from the Epistle to the Hebrews: 'Let us who have so great a cloud of witnesses over our head run with patience the race that is set before us.'

What happened in the dark cell in which Wilfrid was left, a cell that rarely saw the light of day and was unlit at night, takes us straight to the experiences of the apostles as recounted in the Acts of the Apostles. Like them, he prayed and sang praises to God in his prison. His guards heard him singing the psalms without ceasing, following the injunction of St Paul to the Thessalonians to 'pray without ceasing'. We have seen how naturally the singing of the psalms came to him. In the monastery they formed the backbone of the daily office, and he and his people would sing them as they travelled. Having the psalms by heart, Wilfrid was now sustained by them.

His gaolers, hearing the constant singing, looked into his cell to find the darkness as bright as the day. 'Thunderstruck, they terrified others with the tale of his holiness.' So great was his faith, says Eddius, that he could well have been called 'the light of Britain'. Eddius then breaks into a fervent prayer of glory and thanksgiving to God, the true light, for sending and sustaining this illuminator of his century. Columba had such an experience of the uncreated light, and it is a characteristic of the lives of certain saints from the time of the apostles until St Seraphim of Sarov and to the present day.

WILFRID HEALS THE GAOLER'S WIFE

In the early church, the apostles healed the sick as Christ had done during his earthly life. Wilfrid was granted the same gift. Eddius' *Life of Wilfrid* is exceptional in giving so little account of the miraculous. Many lives of the saints consist of a series of rather formal miracle stories and provide little historical detail. Even Bede's life of St Cuthbert builds each chapter around one of the saint's miracles. Eddius gives us a real sense of development in Wilfrid's life against the changing political background, and the few miracles described form a natural part of the story.

One day the gaoler came running to Wilfrid to ask his help. The gaoler's wife had been struck by a sudden convulsion that left her cold and rigid, foaming at the mouth and scarcely able to breathe. Having blessed some water, Wilfrid sprinkled it on her face and, beseeching God to help her, he dropped some gently onto her lips. The woman opened her mouth, took deep breaths and slowly recovered. After this the gaoler, already overawed by the holiness of his charge, went to the king to ask to be relieved of his duty. For the fear of the wrath of God, he said, he could not continue to ill-treat so holy a man.

Furious, the king sent Wilfrid to Dunbar, to be under another sheriff known to be a hard man, and ordered that Wilfrid be kept bound hand and foot. This the sheriff willingly set about doing, but, however hard they tried, his blacksmiths could not get the shackles to fit Wilfrid's wrists and ankles; they were either too tight to fit or simply slipped off. The guards were terrified by this sign and left him unbound. Wilfrid carried on with his continuous prayer, singing psalms and giving thanks to God.

What finally led to his release was a dramatic illness of Queen Irminburga. This happened while she and the king were on a progress through their realm and were staying at the monastery of Coldingham on the east coast. This is the monastery to which St Audrey, the former wife of the king, had first gone on being vested with the monastic veil by Bishop Wilfrid. Audrey had gone on to Ely, and the abbess at the time of this visit was Aebbe, the sister of Oswy and thus Egfrid's aunt. The abbess found the queen near to death, just before dawn. Her muscles were tight and her whole body contorted. Aebbe went straight to the king and gave her opinion of the matter: it was a direct result of their iniquitous treatment of Wilfrid and, in particular, of the queen's abuse of the relics she had taken from him. At the very least these were to be returned and Wilfrid released, ideally to be fully reinstated, but if the king could not bring himself to do this, at least Wilfrid should be allowed to leave the kingdom in freedom.

So Wilfrid was released, and the queen recovered. Wilfrid and his companions made their way to Mercia, where they were met on the road by a nephew of King Aethilred, who begged them to stay with him. Thanking God for finding him a resting place, Wilfrid immediately set up a little monastery. But he was not to be allowed to rest. The Mercian king's wife was Egfrid's sister and she saw to it that Wilfrid was ejected straightaway. Leaving his monks, Wilfrid made his way to Wessex, in the hope of being received by King Centwini. But his queen was the sister of Egfrid's queen and detested Wilfrid.

Driven from Northumbria, Mercia and Wessex, he finally took refuge in the wildest part of Saxon-occupied Britain. Cut off by impenetrable forest to the north and tricky coastline to the south, Sussex became Wilfrid's home for the next five years.

13

The Missionary Bishop (681–686)

WILFRID IN SUSSEX

Wild winds had been responsible for Wilfrid's first visit to Sussex and the natives were unfriendly. This time he was driven there by the wiles of powerful women, and the natives proved much more accommodating. Sussex and Frisia were the two pagan Germanic kingdoms in which Wilfrid found himself. He had not planned to go there on a mission; he was forced there by circumstances outside his control. Once there, he immediately set to work proclaiming the gospel. There is no hesitation or doubt. Someone with so strong and biblical a sense of history would not see these events as 'chance', but as divine providence. Where God placed him, there he worked. Christ did not promise an easy path but said: 'Blessed are you when men shall revile you and persecute you and shall say all manner of evil against you for my sake.'

King Aethilwalh of the South Saxons had been baptized some years before in Mercia, and King Wulfhere of Mercia had been his sponsor. This means that there were good relations between the two kingdoms, with Sussex dependent on the more powerful Mercians. Wulfhere had secured the relationship by giving Aethilwalh the Isle of Wight as a christening present. Aethilwalh's queen, Eafe, was of the royal family of the Hwicce of the Severn valley – a people that, as we have seen, had been Christian for some time.

The acceptance of Wilfrid, an exile from Northumbria – the great rival of Mercian power – had its political implications. It could prove useful in future to the Mercian king to be recognized as protector, through dependent Sussex, of a notable Northumbrian. Aethilwalh's baptism, as part of a treaty agreement between his land and Mercia, might have been no more than a formality. We have no way of knowing the depth of his faith or that of Queen Eafe. Apart from an Irish monk who was living as a hermit, the king and queen were the only Christians in Sussex on Wilfrid's arrival.

They were ruling over a demoralized land whose 7,000 families were suffering from severe famine. For three years before Wilfrid's arrival, no rain had fallen and in their desperation groups of people – as many as 40 or 50 at a time – would go to the top of a cliff, join hands and throw themselves over, dying either by the fall or through drowning.

WILFRID'S APPROACH TO MISSION

Wilfrid had first to ensure his own welcome and security, which he did by giving the king a full and open account of his last few years and the reason for his having to seek refuge. The king was won over by this account, assured him of his loyalty and said that he would not be seduced by any bribe or threat from Wilfrid's enemies. Wilfrid then talked to king and queen of the beauties of the gospel, the greatness and blessedness of God's kingdom, giving them 'milk without guile'. Having won their hearts and given warmth and zest to their dormant faith, he was permitted to address the people.

We can speculate on the motives for the king's support of Wilfrid. Eddius, of course, tells us only of his being won by the sensitive and persuasive preaching of Wilfrid. There is no reason to disbelieve that this was important. The overall impression we gain of Anglo-Saxon royalty is of its openness to the Christian message. Not only did many of them turn to the monastic life – sometimes admittedly as an alternative to the more normal and violent ways of being deposed from the throne – but a significant number voluntarily stepped down from power to conclude their lives as pilgrims. But they had also to consider the political consequences of adopting Christianity and these could be to their advantage. The Church provided an authoritative and ordered structure, a clear pattern of beliefs and ideas, and a well-defined code of behaviour that could be used to enhance the position of the king. This was particularly so as the Church – with its common liturgy, language and body of canon law – would give the newly-converted people easier access to the wider European world.

St Peter had baptized 3,000 people on the day of Pentecost, following his first proclamation of the gospel. He was preaching to devout Jews who had come to Jerusalem for the festival and were thoroughly familiar with the Old Testament Scriptures. They knew of the life of Jesus and his crucifixion. They had to be convinced that what they were witnessing in the apostles' speaking in many tongues was the outpouring of the Spirit that the prophet Joel had foretold. They had to be brought to recognize the Jesus of the parables and miracles as the long-awaited Christ; they had to hear the heart of the gospel – that the crucified Jesus was the Risen Christ. The vocabulary, the ideas, the longing expectation were all there and they could quickly be brought to believe the gospel. Wilfrid was also able to baptize the Saxons in thousands on one day, but only after a long period of teaching and preparation, for he was dealing with polytheists with no knowledge of the Hebrew Scriptures.

The people were gathered together and Wilfrid spoke to them with all his eloquence over the course of many months. He explained the great works of the Lord from the creation at the beginning of time right up to the last judgement. His words were based first on the Gospels, which he knew by heart, but he drew deeply on the Old Testament, which tells how God led his people from their many gods and idols to the worship of the one God, Creator and Sustainer of all things. All this was pertinent to the pagan Saxons.

Wilfrid's preaching culminated in the call of John the Baptist and Christ's own first proclamation: 'Repent, for the kingdom of God is at hand.' He called every one of them to be baptized, fulfilling his Lord's final commandment to 'make disciples of all the nations baptizing them in the name of the Father and of the Son and the Holy Spirit, teaching them to observe all that I have commanded you'.

KINGS AND CONVERSION

Many 'left their idolatry and acknowledged the Almighty God', Eddius tells us. He then makes a very revealing comment. Some, he said, did so freely, but others 'at the king's command'. How genuine was the Christian conviction of those who were baptized at the king's command? This is an immediate question for us. We think of ourselves living in a culture that permits freedom of belief and makes few explicit requirements of us in the matter of our fundamental convictions. The extent to which such freedom is a possibility in any society is a very difficult question, as none of us can approach such matters with an unformed mind. The things that we take for granted as 'obvious' or 'common sense' are largely culturally determined and, in the human world, where motives are complex and often unconscious, a shift from one view of the world to another is never simply a matter of intellectual persuasion. The world view of the pagan Saxon is virtually inaccessible to us and it is difficult to assess the significance of their baptism to those who were baptized at the king's order.

When Constantine adopted Christianity as the official religion of the Roman Empire, the status of the Church changed dramatically and Christians were given a number of privileges. It became advantageous to belong to the Church, and this acted as an additional motive for conversion. For some it was doubtless the sole reason. The changes to the law that occurred under Constantine are well documented. Doubtless there were analogous changes in Sussex at the time of Wilfrid.

But we are dealing with a much smaller, tribal community, in which it would surely have been very surprising not to adhere to the ways of the king. It is perhaps more surprising that the South Saxon people had not already adopted the religion of their king, Aethilwalh, before the arrival of Wilfrid. Mayr-Harting[1] has suggested that this could be because the aristocracy resented the hegemony of Mercia and therefore resisted baptism, the symbol of Aethilwalh's subordination. They were then quickly won over by the cultured, cosmopolitan and well-connected Wilfrid, who was not part of the Mercian overlordship. King Aethilred of Mercia was, in any case, too occupied with Northumbria to continue the relationship with Sussex and Wilfrid had therefore arrived at the 'psychological moment'.

Our sources do not provide sufficient material for us to be certain about motives. But they do sometimes record events that appear to confirm divine approbation or disapproval. On the very day on which the first South Saxons were baptized, a gentle rain began to fall and the parched land was baptized from the heavens.

That year there was a full harvest and the famine was at an end, doubtless a sign that the natural world responded to the fact that the people were now at one with the Creator of all things. But the end of the famine was not only the result of divine action: Wilfrid and his people had taken immediate steps to alleviate the suffering, by sharing their knowledge of sea fishing. The South Saxons used to catch eels, but had no experience of taking fish from the sea. By joining up their small eel-nets, Wilfrid's men made large ones and took a good catch at sea. One third of the first catch was allocated to the poor.

In gratitude for the success of his work, King Aethilwalh gave the Selsey peninsula to Wilfrid. Here he established a monastery, and used it as his episcopal seat for the five years that he acted as bishop of the South Saxons.

WESSEX INVADES SUSSEX

At the end of the five years an exile appeared in Sussex; Cadwalla of the West Saxons. Keen to have the support of Wilfrid, he vowed to be an obedient son, if Wilfrid would be his spiritual father and guide. This Wilfrid did, supporting him in numerous ways, contributing to Cadwalla's ultimate success in gaining the throne of Wessex. Cadwalla is yet another example, so puzzling to most modern notions of piety, of a Germanic king of notable ferocity who ends his life – in this case a very short one – as a devout and newly baptized Christian in Rome.

According to Bede, Cadwalla invaded Sussex, killed King Aethilwalh and ravaged the land with plunder and slaughter while still a 'daring' young man in exile. The church in Sussex was then denied its own bishop and it became dependent on Winchester. As king, Cadwalla attempted to exterminate the entire population of the Isle of Wight, having made an oath that he would dedicate a quarter of the land to the Lord if he were successful. Successful he was and that quarter, amounting to 300 hides, was indeed given to the Church, to Bishop Wilfrid, who put it in the charge of one of his clergy. Wilfrid also left another priest to act as missionary to the pagan people who remained on the island.

These details are not recorded by Eddius and we do not know the dates at which they took place. There was a constant struggle for dominance between neighbouring kingdoms and Wilfrid's work for the Church often took place during wartime. In this case Wilfrid and the Church were to benefit directly from Cadwalla's military success. As we do not know the causes of the conflict, or the extent to which Wilfrid was informed, we are unable to make a judgement about his involvement.

At last Egfrid of Northumbria, Wilfrid's enemy, overstretched himself. Against advice, he confidently marched into battle against the Picts, at Dunnichen Moss near Forfar. The Picts were expecting him and led him straight into a cleverly created ambush. Egfrid perished with many of his men. The year was 685. It was the end of English overlordship of the Picts. The stage was now set for Wilfrid's return to Northumbria.

Note

1 H. Mayr-Harting in M. J. Kitch (ed.), *Studies in Sussex Church History*, pp. 1–17.

Part V

Northumbria and Mercia

14

The Return to Northumbria

PEACE WITH ARCHBISHOP THEODORE (686–687)

Wilfrid did not return to Northumbria immediately on Egfrid's death. The new king Aldfrid clearly needed time to assess the situation. Many of his advisers would have had an interest in keeping Wilfrid away and would have done their best to prevent his return. Wilfrid was also wary about returning until things had been regularized. Vital to his restoration was the peacemaking work of ArchbishopTheodore.

Nearing his own death, Theodore wished to be reconciled and called Wilfrid to a meeting in London in the presence of its bishop, Eorcanwald. Here he asked Wilfrid's forgiveness for the wrongs he had done him in 'consenting to the king's action' of stripping him of his property and sending him into exile. Would that we had a full account of the conversation of these two great bishops, both practical men of action, both learned in theology and the canons of the Church. We have only Eddius' account of this meeting, and his primary interest was to show that Wilfrid had been in the right. But what shines through his account is the way that the Christian gospel inspired the life of both of them: the willingness to repent and the readiness to forgive others.

Theodore took steps to ensure Wilfrid's reinstatement and wrote to all Wilfrid's former enemies and those in power and positions of influence. He asked King Aldfrid to be reconciled to Wilfrid by peace treaty (*sub foedere pacis*). Unfortunately we do not have the text of this letter, but the use of the term 'peace treaty' implies that Theodore envisaged a detailed specification of the structure of the diocese and the responsibilities for the monasteries, with Wilfrid's position clearly defined. It is most unlikely that Theodore would contemplate the abandonment of the new structure, as it clearly better answered the needs of the people and was in line with his overall policy. It would also have caused disruption and led to further strife as the new bishops and their staffs were removed from office.

The monastery of Whitby continued to be an influential centre in the life of the Northumbrian church after the death of Hilda in 680, and Theodore wrote to Abbess Aelffled, daughter of Queen Eanfled, asking her to befriend Wilfrid. Aeffled certainly made a vital intervention on behalf of Wilfrid later in his life and it is likely that she worked behind the scenes at this time to help his return home.

Theodore's letter to King Aethilred of Mercia was immediately successful. He urged him to do his utmost to help, especially as Wilfrid had been labouring among the pagans for the service of God, while bereft of his own property. Aethilred restored to Wilfrid many of his Mercian monasteries and lands.

WILFRID, ABBOT OF LINDISFARNE

King Aldfrid of Northumbria was more circumspect. He had a much more complex and fraught situation to handle. It would have been no easy matter to reinstate Wilfrid and modify the diocesan structure established by Theodore. The people would have become used to the new arrangements, and the new bishops with all their clergy and officials would not have been easily dislodged. In fact Aldfrid insisted on maintaining this basic structure as he was probably advised to do by Theodore. It was best for the smooth running of the church. It was also in the interest of the king as it prevented excessive power accumulating to one bishop, who could become a threat to his authority.

Egfrid waited for a suitable opportunity and this came in 687, the second year of his reign. In this year Eata, who had been installed as Bishop of Hexham on Wilfrid's expulsion, died, as did Cuthbert, the Bishop and Abbot of Lindisfarne. The way was now clear for King Aldfrid to allow Wilfrid to return. Initially Wilfrid took over Lindisfarne for one year.

Cuthbert died as his monks were singing Psalm 59: 'O God thou hast cast us off and hast broken us down; Thou hast been angry and hast had compassion on us.' The priest Herefrith, who was present at the death, observes that these words proved providential, for 'after Cuthbert was buried such a storm of trouble broke out that several monks chose to depart rather than bear the brunt of such danger'.[1] Wilfrid was presumably the cause of this 'storm of trouble'. We can only guess the nature of the problem.

Anyone would have had difficulty filling the place of the loved and revered Cuthbert. He had been elected Bishop of Lindisfarne at a council presided over by Archbishop Theodore and in the presence of King Egfrid. But, despite letters and messengers, Cuthbert refused to budge from his solitary life on Farne. In the end the king himself, together with Bishop Trumwine and a number of other influential people, came to plead with him. They knelt before him in tears, according to Bede. Reluctantly he went before the synod and accepted consecration.

After two years as bishop, Cuthbert felt that his end was near and happily withdrew to his hermitage. So this loved and gentle hermit was succeeded by Wilfrid, the energetic missionary bishop of vast experience and clear views on the monastic life. The Lindisfarne monks were accustomed to an abbot praying for them in his cell, and now they had an abbot who expected ready and full obedience to the rule of St Benedict. It is easy to understand their relief when Eadbert succeeded after one year and 'bound up their wounds'.

THE RETURN TO YORK

Aldfrid restored the monasteries of Hexham and Ripon to Wilfrid. Then he acted more directly and removed Bosa from York so that Wilfrid could return to his original see after so many years of exile.

Good relations were restored, but they were constantly under threat from those who had benefited from Wilfrid's absence. According to Eddius, the main cause of dissension between Wilfrid and the king was the removal of the possessions of the monastery of St Peter at Ripon and its conversion into an episcopal see. Had the king been able to compromise on this, as Ripon more than anywhere else was Wilfrid's spiritual home, then a longer period of cooperation could have held. As it was, Wilfrid was to spend only five years in Northumbria before an impasse was reached and he left to join his friend Aethilred, the King of Mercia.

15

The Years in Mercia (692–703)

Our sources tell us virtually nothing about Wilfrid's years in
Mercia. They were perhaps the most peaceful in Wilfrid's long life.
There were no wars, plagues or famines and no dramatic turning
points or conflicts. There was little therefore to strike a chronicler.
The normal day-to-day work of the church and its leaders were
well enough known to the readers and not worth recording. But,
at the age of 58, Wilfrid was at the height of his powers and one
of the most experienced bishops in Christendom. Knowing his
enormous energy and commitment, we can be sure that his work
was of lasting importance for the people of Mercia. Aethilred
received him warmly, knowing the contribution that he could
make to the development of his kingdom.

BISHOP IN MERCIA

The kingdom of Mercia stretched from the modern Welsh border
in the west to Lincoln and the fens in the east. It was composed of
a number of different Anglian peoples, each with its own sub-
kingdom. They adopted the Christian faith over a period of time.
The Hwicce of the Severn valley and the folk around Hereford
became Christian through the influence of the indigenous British.
This probably happened in other parts of Mercia as well.

The great King Penda, who fought so often against Northumbria, was a pagan. But he was sympathetic to Christians, provided
they practised what they preached: he could not stand hyprocisy.
His son, Peada, became Christian and, in 653, Penda had made
him king of the sub-kingdom of the Middle Angles, a people
settled in the region of Leicester. Wilfrid was to become Bishop of
the Middle Angles, during his time in Mercia.

There were several things that connected Wilfrid with Mercia,
and with the Middle Angles in particular. Peada had married a

daughter of King Oswy, who agreed to the marriage on the condition that Peada became a Christian; the influence of Queen Eanfled was surely at work here. And it was her son, Wilfrid's friend Alchfrid, who had instructed Peada in the faith.

Peada was baptized by the Irish Bishop Finan, who had succeeded Aidan as Abbot of Lindisfarne in 651, Wilfrid's last year at the monastery. Finan sent four outstanding priests to evangelize and baptize the Mercians: an Irishman called Diuma and three Angles including Cedd, the brother of St Chad. When Oswy defeated Penda at the Battle of Winwaed in 655, he became King of Mercia for three years. Diuma became the first Bishop of Mercia during Oswy's rule. We do not know where his see was, but by 669, when Archbishop Theodore made Chad bishop, it was at Lichfield.

This large kingdom, with its different peoples, needed to be divided into a number of dioceses. This was completed in the early 680s, according to the principles consistently applied by Theodore. When Wilfrid arrived in 692, there were five dioceses, with bishops for Worcester, Hereford, the Middle Angles, central Mercia and Lindsey [Lincolnshire]. Bede tells us that Wilfrid became Bishop of the Middle Angles and it is most likely that his see was based on Leicester.

So Wilfrid arrived in a kingdom with a well-established church structure and a pattern of life very close to that of Northumbria, with its Irish, British and English elements. He would have been able to continue with his work as a bishop, much as he had in Northumbria.

Archbishop Theodore had died in 690 and his successor, Bertwald, was not appointed until 692. Once again, as in his first year as bishop, Wilfrid took on the responsibilities of Canterbury. He carried out consecrations of new bishops, notably Oftfor as bishop for the Hwicce people of the Severn valley. Oftfor was one of five students of Hilda at Whitby to become a bishop.

There were existing monasteries in Mercia. We know about the one that was founded at Breedon just before Wilfrid's arrival. It was a daughter house of the monastery at Peterborough and the nobleman who gave the land was clear about its purpose. He made his grant so that they might found a monastery, but they were to ensure that they established a priest there so that he could preach the gospel and baptize the people. The monasteries played an active part in establishing and developing the faith in their locality. Wilfrid was to found a number of his own monasteries to carry out similar work of preaching, teaching, baptizing and supporting the Christian life.

WILFRID'S MONASTERIES

Wilfrid was first of all a monk, with a deep love of the liturgical rhythms of monastic life. He had a profound knowledge of all aspects of liturgical celebration: the music, the iconography, the pattern of the day and the seasons of the year. In Oundle and the other five monasteries that he founded, the people of Mercia would have experienced Christian worship in its full glory. And it is the monasteries that would have set the pattern.

The monastic life was present from the beginning of the Church, and became very important in the fourth century with the end of the persecutions. Denied the 'crown' of martyrdom in the amphitheatres of the empire, committed followers of the gospel sought their crowns in the 'arena' of the desert. Monasticism was particularly strong in Egypt and Palestine and, after St Athanasius wrote his influential life of St Antony, it quickly spread to all parts of the Christian world. A pattern of manual work and prayer life based on the psalms and the recitation of the Scriptures was established from the beginning. One of the issues for all the early monasteries was to maintain a balance between the ideal of the passionate ascetic, who sought union with God through a solitary life of extreme self-denial, and the reality of the need of individuals to have the support of the community. Where there were hermits, who could be either male or female, the normal pattern was for the solitary hermit (literally 'desert-dweller') to be associated with a coenobitic or 'common-life' monastery at which they would receive communion. Normally monastics would be given a blessing to live as hermits only after having proved themselves by some years of communal life.

The hermit's life of absolute dedication has always had an inspirational hold on the Christian imagination, and this was as true of the early Christians of Britain and Ireland and of the newly converted Anglo-Saxons as of the people of Egypt. The Egyptian and Palestinian monks sought their solitary struggle in the desert.

For the Irish, the desert was an isolated island, and for the Gauls a deep forest. The Angle St Guthlac of Crowland found his on a swampy island in the middle of the impenetrable fens. Hermits would sometimes develop particular gifts of insight and foresight and people would travel great distances to consult them. The British bishops who had the disastrous meeting with St Augustine at the River Severn were guided by the advice of a hermit, and people would penetrate the gloomy and dangerous fen to consult St Guthlac. Others crossed the sea to seek St Cuthbert in his isolation on Farne.

But hermits were exceptional, and the more normal monastic way was in community. Cuthbert's friend Herebert spent his whole life alone on an island in the middle of a lake near Carlisle, but Cuthbert himself was in regular communication with the monastery; his solitary prayer life supported by the communal liturgy of his fellow monastics.

Fundamental to the monastic life is the laying aside of all earthly cares so as to concentrate on 'the one thing needful', as our Lord said to Martha. It is difficult to maintain our focus if, like Martha, we are preoccupied with the myriad practical matters of daily life. Owning no goods, the monastic is freed from many of the concerns of those 'in the world'. The unmarried state liberates such a man or woman from the demands of family life. Most difficult is obedience, which strikes at pride, the root of all sins. In Christian thought, pride is the downfall of us all.

Each monastic, whether living alone or in community, would develop a pattern of prayer and penitence, under the guidance of a spiritual elder. They lived an ascetic life in the struggle to be free of the 'passions', the wild beasts who snarled and tore at them in their desert 'arena'. In their continual chanting of the psalms they prayed to be freed from these constant enemies who surround us all.

Patterns of life developed according to the particular genius of the individuals and their monastic community. But underlying this diversity was a fundamental unity. One of Wilfrid's monks could have settled easily into any other monastery in Christendom. Though there were many rules governing the life of the monasteries, the things they had in common were far more numerous and significant than those that separated them.

Wilfrid set up all his monasteries on the basis of the rule of St Benedict. Like Benedict Biscop, he had the advantage of a thorough grounding in the practices of Gaul and Rome. He wished to see that full and rich liturgical, monastic and diocesan life in his own lands, uniting its diverse peoples in a common life and at one with their Christian brothers and sisters in the rest of the Roman patriarchate and the four other patriarchates of the world-wide Church.

CHURCH COUNCILS

One of the mysteries of the seventh century is the whereabouts of Cloveshoe, the town in which Theodore established his annual councils of the whole church. One of the largest and most complete Anglo-Saxon churches in the country stands to this day at Brixworth in Mercia. It was clearly a place of considerable importance, but there is no mention of it in the early records. A case for the identification of Brixworth with Cloveshoe can be made from topography – Brixworth is on a height, a 'hoe', which is cloven like an upturned hoof.[2] There are one or two historical hints to support this. There is a connection of St Boniface of Crediton with Brixworth, and he is known to have had an interest in the canons of the councils of Cloveshoe.

Unfortunately, our records of these councils are very incomplete. But there is every likelihood that Wilfrid, who had represented the whole country at a council of 125 bishops in Rome, was involved in them. He would have played an important part in establishing common canons of daily practice that would last through the following centuries and help to keep all parts of the church in these lands to a common understanding.

Wilfrid, it seems, worked assiduously in Mercia. There is no hint of his pining to return to Northumbria or of resentment at his position. Perhaps he could have finished his long life in peace as bishop in Mercia. But this peaceful time was to end. He was summoned to a council by Archbishop Bertwald.

16

Wilfrid's Enemies Reassemble

THE COUNCIL OF AUSTERFIELD (702)

Theodore was never in direct confrontation with Wilfrid. He gained his long-term ends by taking advantage of the political complexities of his time. His successor, Archbishop Bertwald, apparently worked happily with Wilfrid for the first ten years of his time in Canterbury. Then, suddenly, in 702, Wilfrid was called to a council of the church in Austerfield, near today's Bawtry in Yorkshire.

We do not know the underlying politics that led to this council. It was called to reach a final resolution of the old problems: Wilfrid's jurisdiction and properties in Northumbria. We can only speculate on the reason for this once again becoming an issue. It was not due to any change of the leading characters, as Aldfrid was still king, Bertwald remained archbishop and Bishop Bosa had been reinstalled in York. It is not an edifying story, which is presumably why Bede omits all reference to this council. This leaves Eddius as our only source and, allowing for his overstatement of the iniquity of Wilfrid's enemies, it appears that there were two groups in the renewed opposition: the Northumbrian bishops and the advisers of the king.

As long as the canonical position of the monasteries and dioceses of Northumbria was left unresolved, there remained the potential for dispute. Bishop could more easily come into conflict with abbot. Doubtless the monks of Wilfrid's own monastery in Ripon, who included his biographer Eddius, continued to resent the diminution of their own position and wanted their revered abbot and bishop back.

The various political factions would have been manoeuvring for position at the court of the ageing king, who was soon to die of illness. The counsellors of the king were central to the moves to call the council and summon Wilfrid. The threat of military force lay in the background throughout the discussions. The strategy for managing the meeting had been carefully prepared.

Archbishop Bertwald and nearly all the other bishops were already assembled in Deira. They sent a deputation to Wilfrid requesting him to attend. All the canons would be honoured and he was assured of a safe passage. The early meetings were stormy. It seems that the Northumbrian bishops were emphatic, if not confrontational, about the authority of their new sees. After 40 years as a bishop, Wilfrid was being judged by those much younger and less experienced and some of them were running his former diocese.

According to Eddius, some of the bishops were driven by avarice. This may be a partisan slur, but it is not at all unlikely that some of them were more interested in enjoying the fruits of office than in carrying out their duty. In a letter he wrote to Egbert 30 years later, Bede referred to such bishops, who made sure that their revenues were collected from even the most isolated communities, but never visited them, leaving them unbaptized 'like sheep without a pastor'. If there were such bishops at the council, it is easy to see how someone as absolutely committed, energetic and thoroughgoing as Wilfrid would be offended.

Wilfrid was asked to accept all the decrees of Archbishop Theodore. He replied that he was willing to obey in every respect provided all was in conformity with canon law. It was at this point that one of the king's officers disguised himself and stole out of his tent. He mingled with the crowd and came secretly to Wilfrid to warn him.

A TRAP

This officer owed his life to Wilfrid, who had taken him in as a helpless infant and brought him up. Devoted to the bishop, who had been a true father to him, this man now revealed the underlying strategy of those who were managing the council. Their plan, it appears, was to get Wilfrid to sign an apparently innocuous document. Later he would discover that he had agreed to handing over all his rights in Northumbria and Mercia, so that neither monastery, nor diocese, nor any other property would be left to him. He would even have agreed to his own deposition as bishop. It is difficult to believe that Wilfrid would have agreed to sign anything that could be used in this way but, forewarned, he was more wary from then on.

The council demanded an immediate reply, but Wilfrid said that he needed first to see the nature of the archbishop's decision. He said again that he would wholeheartedly follow it, provided it conformed to the decisions of the holy fathers. The upshot was that their real demands were openly revealed. They had a fallback position, which was to offer Wilfrid full rights as Abbot of Ripon, his own and first monastery, to which all former possessions would be returned, provided he relinquish his position as bishop. At this point Wilfrid was driven to justify all he had done in Northumbria.

WILFRID JUSTIFIES HIMSELF

Had Wilfrid not been the first to rid Northumbria of its Scottish customs? Had he not brought the whole kingdom into unity with the rest of Christendom over the celebration of Easter? Was it not he who had taught all the churches the beautiful practice of antiphonal singing in the traditional ways perfected in the continental churches? Was he not the one who had introduced the Rule of St Benedict to the monasteries? And now, having been told of no offence that he had committed, and being unaware of any crime, he was being asked to condemn himself, even to the violation of his holy office as bishop. With every confidence he said he would appeal to the Holy See.

Anglo-Saxon kings were not accustomed to being thwarted. The appeal to a superior authority within the Church must often have galled them. Wilfrid stood condemned in the eyes of King Aldfrid for preferring the judgement of Rome to his own, and he offered his army to force Wilfrid to submit. But this went too far for the bishops. They reminded the king of the promise of safe conduct and that Wilfrid never would have come without it.

So Wilfrid was able to return to Aethilred in safety. Perhaps he could have resumed his former position as Bishop of Mercia, had the whole situation not been embittered by the events at

Austerfield. His followers were virtually excommunicated. If any of his abbots or priests were to bless the food at table, everything was to be thrown away as if offered to idols.

On his return he recounted the unhappy saga to Aethilred and asked where he now stood in Mercia. The king confirmed that all his former grants and conditions still held. With this assurance Wilfrid embarked on his second appeal to Rome.

17

Wilfrid's Last Journey to Rome (703–704)

THE APPEAL

Once he had crossed the channel, despite being in his late sixties, Wilfrid made the journey to Rome on foot. Unlike his previous continental travels, this one was troubled by neither storm nor murderous enemies and Wilfrid was able to present his appeal to Pope John in writing. The text forms Chapter 51 of Eddius' *Life of Wilfrid*.

It is a fascinating document. On the one hand it shows Wilfrid's willingness to accept the decisions of the Holy See. If, he said, even the smallest accusation of his opponents was found to 'hold water' he would gladly submit to the judgement of the Pope. On the other hand, it reveals Wilfrid as an experienced bishop, confidently addressing a fellow bishop and advising him on possible ways forward. He outlines the procedure that he expects the Pope to follow: to confirm all the decrees of his predecessor Agatho relating to his case; to require anyone coming with accusations against him to make them openly in his presence; and to allow him to reply to them. He then asks the Pope to write to the kings of Mercia and Northumbria. He requests that King Aethilred be told of his well-being and asked to adhere to the directions of previous popes relating to the monasteries that Aethilred and his brother Wulfhere had given Wilfrid 'for their souls' salvation'; nobody 'through foul greed or envy' was to lay hands on them.

But it is his advice on what the Pope was to write to King Aldfrid that is most revealing of Wilfrid's thinking. He asks him to address the king in 'very quiet diplomatic terms' to follow the decrees of Pope Agatho relating to Northumbria, but 'if this should go against the grain with him, because of my part in the business' then Pope John should decide who is best fitted to govern the see of York and all its many monasteries. What Wilfrid is not prepared to give up are the houses of Hexham and Ripon and their attendant properties, which were granted to him by Agatho in a single privilege. The rigorous upholder of correct procedure here shows himself willing to compromise, to forego the great see of York, soon to be recognized as an archbishopric in accordance with the original directions of Gregory the Great, in return for his greatest treasure, the monastery at Ripon.

Wilfrid concludes by saying that he had always shown respect and fraternal charity towards Archbishop Bertwald and would continue to do so and expected him to carry out the decrees of Agatho. So he begins and ends by directing the Pope to the decisions of his predecessor.

THE CASE AGAINST WILFRID

After Archbishop Bertwald's envoys had presented their charges against Wilfrid, Pope John told the synodal court that they needed to consider what Agatho, Benedict and Sergius, his predecesors, thought of the matter, and then to come to the present dispute. A day was set for the hearing.

On that day Archbishop Bertwald's representatives were given leave to present any of their charges to start with and then to proceed to the others. Their main charge was that Wilfrid had 'contumaciously despised and rejected' the statutes of Bertwald in front of the whole synod. To this Wilfrid replied that he had promised the synod his 'wholehearted assent' to everything laid down by the archbishop 'as long as it tallied with the rules and statutes of the holy fathers and with the canonical definitions'. The sticking point was that Wilfrid had been expected to sign his assent before knowing the content of the document that he was asked to sign. This 'rigid and narrow' constraint clearly was impossible to accept; he might be assenting to things impossible to fulfil.

THE ROMAN SYNOD SIFTS THE EVIDENCE

Having heard charge and defence, the fathers of the council had a long discussion among themselves – in Greek. The Pope and many of his people at this time were Greeks. Wilfrid and his priests and deacons had not had the advantage of attending Archbishop Theodore's school at Canterbury, so they were unable to follow the discussion. What a pity that one of the younger Canterbury-educated clergy of Britain, able to speak Greek as well as Latin, was not in Wilfrid's party. We might then have known what they were discussing. Whatever it was, they found some amusement in it, for they were smiling among themselves.

Reporting back on their discussion, they said that they would diverge from the normal procedure. When a number of charges were brought, the accepted procedure was not to proceed with any of the others if the first one could not be proved. In this case, however, out of respect for the archbishop and in reverence to Bishop Wilfrid – 'who had been so long fraudulently despoiled' – they would sift through all the charges over the course of weeks and months, so that the matter could be resolved once and for all.

This first hearing was sufficient for Wilfrid to know that he had been vindicated in the essentials, and he returned with his people to his lodgings to prepare for the coming hearings. His accusers returned home.

Whatever the Greek fathers of the council had found to smile about, they were not treating the matter lightly. Seventy sessions were held over the course of four months to consider the issues, and Wilfrid was 'refined in a veritable furnace of cross-examination'.

One of the most telling moments of the sessions occurred when the documents of the synod held under Agatho were read out:

> Wilfrid, Bishop of the city of York, having appealed to the Apostolic See and having been cleared by the same authority of certain definite and indefinite charges, did, together with one hundred and twenty-five of his fellow-bishops in this synod and judgement seat, confess the true and Catholic faith on behalf of all the northern part of Britain and Ireland and the islands inhabited by the Angles, Britons, Picts and Scots, and did corroborate the same with his signature.

This struck the members of the synod with amazement. Here they were, sitting in judgement on a venerable bishop, who had been a respected member of a famous council of the Church that had met a quarter of a century before. And when a certain Boniface spoke up on behalf of this man who had been a bishop for 40 years, the stage was set for the Pope to give his final summing up.

'We have examined', he said, 'the case of the blessed Bishop Wilfrid, whom God loves, in numerous sessions of this council, and we can find nothing against him. Therefore, by the authority of St Peter, in whom resides the power of binding and loosing from secret sins, we declare him acquitted.' He went on to say that the synod confirmed the decrees of Agatho, Benedict and Sergius, the former popes, which had been delivered to the kings and archbishop in the past.

We know about the discussions of the synod and their final decision from the long letter sent by the Pope to the kings of Mercia and Northumbria, which is recorded in Chapter 54 of Eddius' *Life of Wilfrid*. They had received a detailed written document from Wilfrid and they had read the many accusations against him. Having considered the whole history of the case in detail, they had cross-examined Wilfrid closely. They had also heard from former close acquaintances of his in Rome. One might have expected a detailed list of decrees specifying exactly the extent and nature of Wilfrid's properties and of his rights as Bishop of York. Nothing of the sort. The whole matter is referred for detailed decision at the local level. Bertwald and Wilfrid are to convene a local synod, they are to listen carefully to the submissions of bishops Bosa and John and are to make their own decisions. Only if they fail to reach a resolution are they to have recourse to Rome and then both parties are to attend. If anyone does not deign to come, he is to be removed from office.

Cleared of all charges, the elderly Wilfrid had only one wish, to remain and end his days in the Holy City. This was not to be. The Pope and synod ordered him to return to present their findings to the kings and the archbishop, to heal the suffering of his people and to give his friends cause to rejoice. All this was to be achieved in the last five years of his life, but only after an arduous return journey.

18

Reconciliation

WILFRID NEAR DEATH

To travel back to Britain from Rome was a demanding journey for a man of 70. Eddius' account, with its reference to rough paths and mountainous ways, gives a sense of the effort required. Although lacking the dramatic events of his previous journeys, he very nearly died on the way. He was taken seriously ill in Gaul and was carried unconscious in a litter into the town of Meaux. He ate nothing for four days. On the morning of the fifth day, as dawn was breaking, he was visited by the Archangel Michael in shining raiment. The intercessions of the blessed Virgin and the tears of his followers had been heard, the angel said, and several years had been added to his life so that he would end his days in peace in his native land. He had built churches in honour of the apostles Andrew and Peter, but none dedicated to the Blessed Mary, Ever-Virgin, who had been interceding for him. He was ordered to put this right on his return. 'I will visit you in four years. Be prepared.'

WELCOME IN CANTERBURY, LONDON AND MERCIA

Wilfrid recovered and, after an easy crossing, reached safe harbour in Kent. He went straight to archbishop Bertwald and good relations were immediately established. The speed with which this happened confirms the suspicion that the archbishop had been under great political pressure from King Aldfrid at the time of the council of Austerfield. Aldfrid was to remain implacably opposed to Wilfrid until shortly before his death.

By this time Wilfrid had been joined by many of the abbots of his monasteries, who had heard the good news of his return, and, laden with presents, he made a joyful progress to London. From there he went on to his loyal friend Aethilred of Mercia, who was overcome with tears as they embraced. Not only did he agree immediately to all the requirements of the letter from the Roman synod, but he also summoned his appointed heir, Coenred, and made him swear to uphold all the decisions of the Roman see.

REJECTION IN NORTHUMBRIA

It was not going to be so easy to approach King Aldfrid. Wilfrid listened carefully to the advice of Aethilred on this and made a careful selection of people to form a delegation to the Northumbrian court. Their respectful approach met with a courteous response from the king, who said he would give careful consideration to their request that Wilfrid visit him in person to present the findings of the Roman synod. On the day appointed for his response he was again courteous, saying that he would grant them anything they asked, but 'Pester me no more with this business of your master Wilfrid.' As far as he was concerned the decision had been made long before by his predecessors and Archbishop Bertwald, and virtually all the bishops of Britain had concurred. No document from the Holy See would make him change his mind.

It would have been hard work to have to unscramble rights to properties, when things had at last settled down. It is very likely that, as Eddius suggests, Aldfrid was persuaded by his counsellors. They would doubtless have included those who had benefited from the re-allocation of Wilfrid's lands. But Aldfrid was nearing the end of a 20-year reign and it is easy to see why he did not wish to be 'pestered' with these old problems.

As Wilfrid's delegation returned with the sad news, Aldfrid was suddenly struck down with a serious illness. He saw this as divine retribution for his intransigence and vowed to carry out the decrees of Rome to the letter. 'If only Wilfrid would come to me now,' he said, 'I would quickly make amends.' If he should die he bid his successor to come to terms with Wilfrid for the good of both their souls. The authority for these final words of Aldfrid, the illegitimate son of King Oswy, was his half-sister, Abbess Aelffled, the daughter of the great Queen Eanfled. The mother had set Wilfrid off on the first steps of his long journey: the daughter was to be important as he approached his final home.

Aldfrid was not to live. Five days after his change of heart he was dead, to be succeeded by Eadwulf.

A PALACE REVOLT

Wilfrid was at Ripon with Eadwulf's young son and immediately made friendly overtures to the new king. These were violently repulsed. Wilfrid was given six days to be out of Northumbria on pain of death for himself and all his followers. The extreme violence of this response suggests that Eadwulf and his counsellors had particular reason to fear Wilfrid's return, and it appears that there was a deep-seated insecurity in his political situation. After only two months on the throne, Eadwulf was driven out, to be replaced by Aldfrid's infant son Osred, who became the adopted son of Wilfrid.

Our sources do not enlighten us on the nature of the conspiracy that ousted Eadwulf. The royal Abbess Aelffled could well have been an influential party to the plot. Several recent historians have seen Wilfrid's hand at work behind the scenes. This is not impossible, given the range of his contacts, his great popularity in many quarters and his vast experience of influencing those in high places for the advancement of the Christian faith.

THE COUNCIL IN NIDDERDALE (706)

The political conditions favourable, Archbishop Bertwald lost no time in carrying out the decrees of Rome. He travelled north, called the king and all his leading people, together with all the bishops and abbots, to a synod on the east bank of the river Nidd. He arrived on the same day as Wilfrid.

The proceedings were opened by the archbishop reading the documents sent by the Holy See. When he had completed the reading there was complete silence. Had anyone understood the sophisticated Latin of the Roman texts? Certainly Bertfrid, the nobleman ruling during the young king's minority, had not. 'Those of us who could not follow the reading would be grateful if you would explain just what the Holy See means,' he said. Tactfully, the archbishop agreed that the 'papal pronouncements are couched in obscure and roundabout terms' and proceeded to give the gist of the texts. This was that all should, as they valued their own salvation, be reconciled to Wilfrid once and for all, and that Wilfrid be given back all his former jurisdiction.

Exact boundaries would be a matter of contention and the extent of Wilfrid's jurisdiction had varied over the many years of his episcopate, as a result of the military fortunes of Northumbria. Archbishop Bertwald dealt with this by saying that he himself, with the help of prudent advisers, would determine their exact extent. Interestingly it was the bishops who objected. They appealed to the decisions of Archbishop Theodore and King Egfrid, which Aldfrid and the archbishop himself had confirmed at Austerfield.

At this point Abbess Aelffled made her stunning contribution. She revealed to the council the deathbed will and testament of Aldfrid in which he promised, if he were to live, to fulfil all the demands of the Holy See regarding Wilfrid. If he were to die, he bid his son and heir to do likewise.

This led the regent Bertfrid to tell the assembly of an extraordinary event when his forces were besieged and in a hopeless situation at Bamburgh. They made a vow that if God would grant the young prince his father's kingdom, they would carry out all the Pope's injunctions concerning Bishop Wilfrid. No sooner had they made this vow than the enemy ceased hostilities and rushed up to greet them. 'The king and the earls will that the command of the Holy See and King Aldfrid's instructions be followed to the last detail.'

This made the bishops think again. Abbess Aelffled gave her advice and the archbishop his. A resolution was agreed by all parties. Wilfrid was to get back Ripon and Hexham with all their revenues. This realistic compromise would not disturb the basic structure of Archbishop Theodore's settlement and conformed to Wilfrid's own fallback position. The situation was resolved more easily because, in the same year as the council of Nidd, Bosa, Bishop of York, died and was succeeded by the saintly John who until then had been Bishop of Hexham. But there would have been a number who would have had to relinquish tenure in those of Wilfrid's properties that were to be returned.

Finally after 30 years, all parties were reconciled. They brought down Christ's peace upon themselves, says Eddius.

19

Last Instructions (709)

With joy Wilfrid started to make his way to Hexham. But he was laid low with the same malady that had struck him at Meaux, in a yet more severe form. The four years promised him by the Archangel Michael were up. The news spread rapidly and his abbots and many isolated hermits came from all over the country to be at his deathbed. They all knelt, beseeching God to remember his promise that 'when two or three are gathered together in my name there am I in the midst of them'. Their prayer was answered and the bishop recovered, lived for a further 18 months and had time to put everything in due order.

Wilfrid summoned two of his abbots and six of his most faithful friends to Ripon to act as witnesses to his last will and oversee the distribution of the many gifts that he had been given over the course of his life. He asked them to arrange all the precious stones, gold and silver in four separate piles, he himself deciding into which pile each should go. One pile was to go to Rome for the support of the churches of the Mother of the Lord and St Paul's. It had been his intention, he said, to go on a final pilgrimage to Rome in order to take the gifts himself and to end his days there. Now that God had disposed otherwise and that he was to die in his own land, he asked his companions to send the gifts for him.

One quarter of his wealth was to go to support the poor of his diocese. The protection of the poor, the widow and orphan are central biblical commandments. To care for the poor was to show love for Christ himself; 'As you did it to one of the least of my brethren, you did it to me,' says our Lord in the parable of the sheep and the goats.

Another quarter was to be given to his beloved monasteries at Ripon and Hexham so that they would have the wherewithal in their dealings with bishops and kings. The last part was to be given to those who shared his long years of exile. Some of these he had already rewarded with lands and this last quarter was to go to the rest, according to their need, so that none should go without.

He had then to arrange for the governance of his monasteries before the Archangel Michael came to fetch him. The 'signs of death are crowding thick about me', he said as he rested to gain strength for this, his final work. One of those present among his closest friends was his kinsman, the priest Tatbert. Wilfrid made him Abbot of Ripon, to rule jointly with him until his death and to be in sole command when he died. Having made this crucial appointment, Wilfrid had a bell rung to summon the whole community, to hear his final decisions.

He began with brother Caelin, who had been an example to all in his observance of the monastic rule. Wilfrid gave his blessing for Caelin to return to his earlier life as a hermit, to live in the wild parts of the country and give himself up to solitary contemplation. Here we see Wilfrid following ancient monastic tradition. The monk had proved himself able to live according to the rule of the communal monastery, and had sufficiently conquered the passions to be allowed to attempt the much more arduous struggle of the solitary life.

Wilfrid then told his community that he would be accompanying the abbots Tibba and Ebba to Mercia. King Coelred wished to confer with him and to make him his director in the Christian life. Urging them to keep the rule, he said that should he not return, they were to accept as abbot whomsoever was chosen by his witnesses, Tibba, Ebba, the priest Tatbert and the others. His beloved community at Ripon was never again to see him alive.

On reaching Mercia, Wilfrid went around all his monasteries, making final arrangements and ensuring that each had the necessary endowments. A few of his abbots were told the full details of his will and all were given his final advice and blessing. One day, when out riding with his kinsman Tatbert, he gave him a full account of his life. This would have been a major source for Eddius' work. His final stay was at Oundle and one of his last acts was to grant Hexham Abbey to Acca. Acca succeeded Wilfrid in the see and, with Tatbert, Abbot of Ripon, caused Eddius to compose the life of their great bishop.

Having completed all these arrangements, Wilfrid blessed the whole community and lay quietly back on his pillow. The brethren chanted the psalms around his bed day and night, weeping as they sang. When they reached the verse of Psalm 103 that says, 'Send forth Thy spirit and they shall be created and Thou shalt renew the face of the earth', Wilfrid breathed his last and there was a sound in the air like a flight of birds approaching.

Notes

1 Bede, *Life of Cuthbert*, ch. 40.
2 There is a discussion about the whereabouts of Cloveshoe in Simon Keynes, *The Councils of Cloveshoe*, Vaughan Paper No. 38, University of Leicester, 1993.

Part VI

Conflicts and Controversies

20

Wilfrid and the Historians

The first life of St Wilfrid was written soon after his death by one of his monks, Eddius Stephanus, to whose work reference has already often been made here. He was passionate and partisan, and gives a scathing portrayal of Wilfrid's opponents. His *Life of Wilfrid* was the first historical biography to be written in England. In chronological sequence, Eddius recorded all the main events in the life of Wilfrid and portrayed him in the thick of the political complexities and conflicts of the time.

Bede drew on this work, but his account of Wilfrid is measured and rather cool, in contrast to his warm and enthusiastic portrayal of the Irish saint Aidan. Given his disapproval of Irish customs, which Wilfrid had done so much to change, one would have expected Bede to be more positive. There are various theories about this. Bede's use of Eddius and his view of Wilfrid remain matters of academic debate.[1]

Modern perceptions of Wilfrid are still coloured by the roles he has been made to play in later controversies. Protestant writers have tried to show that the early church in Britain was independent of the papacy, and Wilfrid, with his appeals to Rome, was not helpful to their case. At best, his importance is understated; at worst he is pilloried for his arrogant abuse of power. 'It appears plainly,' says Thomas Carte in his *General History of England*, written in 1747,

> that he was very fond of himself; had a great opinion of his own parts and merits; and was too much elated by the success of his labours . . . He loved wealth, power, state, pomp and splendour; perhaps the effect of his natural disposition and of a certain haughtiness of mind; but certainly much confirmed by his foreign education; to which, and to the maxims he had imbibed at Rome, all the troubles of his life were owing.

There are hints of treachery here, that an Englishman should allow his education to be adulterated by foreign influence, and even worse, that it should be Roman!

Such excesses were answered by Roman apologists in the nineteenth century. Some of these were careful and scholarly, but it is the more flamboyant accounts that tend to be remembered. They create an even less favourable image of Wilfrid in the popular mind. In his *Life of St Wilfrid* written in 1844, one of the short-lived series of Newman's *Lives of the English Saints*, Faber says of Wilfrid that 'he materially aided the blessed work of riveting more tightly the happy chains which held England to St Peter's chair . . . he rescued England . . . from the wretched and debasing formality of nationalism'. Faber maintained that, at Whitby, Wilfrid 'laid open the true disease of England', its 'stubborn non-conformity' which 'plunged it into the depth of sacrilege, heresy and libertinism, in which it has lain since the time of Henry the Eighth'.

From the other side of the Roman Catholic–Protestant divide, we can read the lecture given in St Paul's Cathedral in 1896 by G. F. Browne,[2] which he prefaced with the words:

> This subject would have been a very thorny one at any time of our history since the commencement of the fight for restored freedom which culminated in the Reformation. The modern aggression of the Roman schism makes it a very thorny subject indeed just now.

It has been suggested[3] that it took the work of Wilhelm Levison, an expatriate German Jew writing in the 1930s and 1940s, to give us a more balanced picture after these rival versions of the nineteenth and early twentieth centuries.

The pugnacity of Eddius, the coolness of Bede, the conflicts in which Wilfrid was involved and the anachronistic use made of his life by polemicists in later controversies have left a number of negative pictures. Wilfrid has been charged with being interested in wealth and power and with dealing with his opponents in a haughty and confrontational manner.

21

Wealth and Poverty

Let us deal first with the charge that Wilfrid was interested in wealth. He was given large donations throughout his life. These were not for his personal use, but for the Church. The fact that they were so generous is a sign of confidence in his integrity. Kings gave him land, knowing that the income would be properly used to build churches and monasteries.

Most of this wealth provided endowments to secure the future of these buildings and institutions. Future generations were able more easily to hear the gospel and glorify God because of Wilfrid's economic and political realism. The fact that he expected and provided for the highest standards of workmanship was costly, but ensured that his buildings remained for the future. Paulinus' church at York was in a ruinous state within 40 years of building. Wilfrid rebuilt it to the highest specifications and secured the necessary endowments to sustain it. The Gospel Book at Ripon was written in gold on empurpled parchment for the glory of God, but also so that it would last for centuries to come. His bequest to the abbots of Hexham and Ripon so that they had 'something in hand to secure the favour of kings and bishops' was the decision of a man only too familiar with political reality.

But these endowments were also for the support of future generations of the poor, the orphaned and the widowed. He left one quarter of his final estate for the continued relief of the poor and his disciples followed his example. Acca annually gave away one tenth of his property to the poor. The fact that he did so on the anniversary of Wilfrid's death is a telling tribute.

Wilfrid's ideal was to live as a simple monk. The most joyful part of Eddius' story is Wilfrid's time in solitary confinement when thrown into prison by King Egfrid. Stripped of all possessions and without the burden of administrative responsibilities, he was able to spend day and night singing psalms and praising God.

An Anglo-Saxon king was generous with his hoard of treasure during his life. At death his dragon-guarded burial-barrow was filled with finely wrought golden torques and precious stones, the visible evidence of his greatness. True to his Germanic origins, Wilfrid too was generous with the treasures given him. But in death no hoard was buried with him. The treasures left to posterity were the many communities he had founded, the great buildings, the illuminated manuscripts, the rich traditions of liturgical chant, the miracle-working relics and the long-term support of the poor and needy.

22

Authority and Obedience

A second charge made against Wilfrid is his alleged love of power leading to disputes over his position and property. He was certainly concerned about his episcopal rights and monastic properties, and about proper canonical order for the sake of the stability of the Church. Had Wilfrid been interested in power and personal aggrandisement, he had a number of opportunities to grasp the highest positions.

Gregory the Great had a clear vision for the organization of the church in Britain, the details of which are spelt out in a letter to Augustine. He envisaged Augustine as the Metropolitan Bishop of London and authorized him to consecrate twelve bishops for the province. He was also to consecrate a bishop for the city of York and if in time the people 'in the adjoining territory accept the word of God', the Bishop of York was to consecrate twelve other bishops and 'hold the dignity of Metropolitan'. He was to remain subject to Augustine's authority while he lived, but afterwards he was to preside over his province and be independent of the Bishop of London. From then onwards, precedence was to depend on seniority of consecration.

Canterbury, of course, took the place of London, but the Roman patriarchate retained this view of the basic structure. When Pope Honorius heard of Bishop Paulinus' success in Northumbria, he sent him the '*pallium*' that conferred metropolitan status and explained in detail the nature of his relationship, as Bishop of York, to the Metropolitan Bishop of Canterbury. Either of them could consecrate the successor to the other. All this he spelt out not only to Paulinus but also in a letter to King Edwin. This took place in 634, the year of Wilfrid's birth. A Bishop of York interested in status could have proclaimed himself Metropolitan Bishop of York, in line with Gregory the Great's instructions.

Attempts have been made to interpret the dispute with Theodore as a conflict over the powers of York vis-à-vis Canterbury, but they fail because there is no evidence that Wilfrid ever made such a claim. Status for its own sake held no attractions for him. When Theodore, at their last meeting, suggested that Wilfrid succeed him at Canterbury, he displayed no interest. He simply observed that the decision was in the hands of the synod.

Certainly Wilfrid knew how to use power. He had, after all, been schooled in Rome and Lyon and had seen how their bishops exercised authority like patrician Romans. But his earliest experiences were at Lindisfarne, and his life as a bishop in Northumbria and Mercia was in many ways closer to that of Columba, or one of the other Irish abbots, leading a scattered commonwealth of many monasteries.

As a young man, Wilfrid's life was characterized by obedience to his parents, to Cudda, to Queen Eanfled and to his 'father' Annemund. His later life was marked by his obedience to the gospel and the canons of the Church. His people loved him and supported him. It was his wholehearted obedience that was the ultimate source of his authority.

23

Ethnicity and Orthodoxy

Wilfrid's commitment to orthodox practice is the source of two rather different criticisms. The first is from those English Protestants who believe that his appeals to Rome helped to make England subservient to a foreign power and her church subordinate to an outsider. The second dates from a nineteenth-century, romantic view of the Celts that has been in vogue again in recent years. According to this view, Wilfrid was largely responsible for the elimination of the 'Celtic church' from the parts of Britain controlled by the Anglo-Saxons.

BRITAIN AND ROME

The main disputes in Wilfrid's life led to appeals to Rome, a fact that riled King Aldfrid. 'Let him stand condemned for preferring their judgement to ours,' he said.

In the case of a dispute involving a bishop, appeal would normally be made to other local bishops, or to the provincial bishop. In a dispute involving a metropolitan bishop, appeal would be made to the patriarch. Wilfrid's dispute with Theodore had to go to Rome.

The bishops of major towns had jurisdictional authority over their province. Rome, the capital of the Empire, naturally had a certain pre-eminence. More important in the eyes of the faithful was the fact that the two chief apostles – Peter and Paul – were martyred here. From the second century, churches were built on the sites of the martyrs and, wherever possible, housed their relics, which were much visited by pilgrims. Rome became one of the more important centres of pilgrimage.

The authority of the Bishop of Rome within the area of his jurisdiction was the same as that of the Pope of Alexandria in his, or that of the Patriarch of Constantinople within his patriarchate. There was no essential difference. But gradually a Roman theology of the papacy grew up that gave the Pope of Rome a unique position as the 'heir' of St Peter. This way of thinking, based on inheritance law in the Roman legal system, was never accepted by the other four patriarchates, and always had its opponents in the West. It reached a climax in the thirteenth century and was largely responsible for the collapse of the unity of western Christendom in the sixteenth century.

In the seventh century, such thinking was in its infancy. Had Wilfrid been in Asia Minor, he would have appealed to Constantinople. A bishop in his position in Syria would have appealed to Antioch. Those Protestant historians who posit an early British church independent of Rome castigate Wilfrid for seeking to bring Britain into subservience to the Pope. They are as far from the mark as those Roman Catholics, like Faber, who use Wilfrid's appeal to Rome as evidence for a full-blown doctrine of papal primacy in the seventh century.

Wilfrid appealed to Pope Agatho because of the disregard of the canons in his deposition and the appointment of three bishops in his place. But his appeal makes it clear that he is quite prepared to see his diocese divided if that is considered to be for the best. The same is true of his second appeal, in which he offered to relinquish his main see of York, retaining only Ripon and Hexham. His appeal is not against the loss of power or possessions, but against the breaking of ecclesiastical law.

Nobody understood better than Wilfrid the positive role that royalty could play in the life of the Church. He had also seen the damage done when kings interfered with the running of the Church. He had seen his 'father' Annemund martyred, and was in Rome as Pope Martin was dying at the hands of the Byzantine emperor. But his appeals to Rome were against breaches of canon law by the archbishop, not against the decisions of the king.

Wilfrid made no appeal when kept from his see by King Oswy, but went quietly about his work as Abbot of Ripon, acting as bishop when called upon to do so. No appeal was made when relations with King Aldfrid deteriorated so that he had to live in exile: he spent those 12 years constructively in Mercia. Only when Archbishop Theodore cooperated with King Egfrid's decisions

112

and acted against the canons did Wilfrid appeal to Pope Agatho. Only when summoned to Austerfield and asked to act against the decrees of the Pope by King Aldfrid, with the support of Archbishop Bertwald, did Wilfrid appeal to Pope John.

Ultimately an evaluation of these appeals will depend on the view taken of the importance of ecclesiastical order. There was a unity of practice and of theological understanding in the seventh century that is difficult for us to appreciate. It was possible for those holding the office of bishop to be an Irishman in Gaul, a Syrian in Rome and a Greek in Britain because there was a shared understanding of the Church, of her teachings and order. The fulness of the unity in Christ was expressed in all aspects of church life and any departure from this due order was dangerous.

WILFRID AND THE IRISH

What about Wilfrid and the Celts? The main issue was the date of Easter. The calculation of the date of Easter is notoriously complex. The Irish and British method of calculation meant that the resurrection could fall on the first Sunday between the 14th and the 21st day of the moon, whereas the Roman dating gave a range from the 15th to the 21st. This means that the resurrection could be celebrated by the British and Irish on the same day as the Jewish passover, the 14th of the month Nisan. This does not make them *quartodecimans*, who always celebrated Easter on the fourteenth, whatever day of the week that happened to be, because the resurrection in the Celtic tradition was always celebrated on a Sunday, the first day of the week. But their practice did not follow the Council of Nicaea, which required that the resurrection, the 'New Pascha', should always fall after the Jewish Passover.

There are two reasons why this question is important. First is the theological significance of the date. Christians live a life transfigured by the incarnation, life, death and resurrection of Christ the co-eternal Son of God. These events all took place at particular times in a particular period of history. The liturgical seasons reflect the great events in the life of the Saviour, and times and dates therefore carry the gospel message. This is particularly true of the resurrection, the central event in the Christian life. The unity of the Church, the body of Christ, is celebrated above all on this joyful festival of the overcoming of death and the opening up of the kingdom of God to all. To celebrate it at different times is an affront, almost a denial of these central Christian truths.

The second reason follows from this and has to do with the unity of the Church, past, present and worldwide. For Colman, it was important to remain at one with St Columba and the holy tradition of Iona. For Wilfrid, it was clear that the church in these islands on the edge of the Christian world had not kept fully in touch with the decisions of the ecumenical councils and the practice of the universal Church.

In holding this position so firmly, Wilfrid was at one with most of the Irish. The question had arisen some time before in the south of Ireland and a deputation had visited Rome to discover the practice there. They were overwhelmed to find that they were out of step not simply with Roman practice, but also with the Greeks, the Egyptians and all other Christians. On their return, they had little difficulty in persuading their countrymen of the need to change. They came to be called *Romani* in contrast to the 'Hibernians' of the north, who adopted the Orthodox date 20 years later.

Wilfrid played a part in bringing all the Northumbrians into line with the the the rest of Christendom, including the majority of the Irish. The monasteries ruled by Iona clung to their old ways for another 50 years before finally adopting the Orthodox date of Easter.

The meeting at St Hilda's monastery in Whitby in 664 is sometimes presented as the occasion on which indigenous 'Celtic'customs were rooted out, to be replaced by those of Rome, and many of the Irish were obliged to leave. This is to state things in terms that are too crudely ethnic. Certainly the decisions made at Whitby had immediate consequences. Bishop Colman and many of his monks, both Irish and English, left Britain for Ireland and established a monastery on the island of Inishbofin. According to Bede, 'all the Scots then living among the English' later conformed or, like Colman, 'returned to their own land'.

Many of those who conformed nevertheless maintained their close links with Ireland and Irish traditions of learning. This was true of Hilda and the monastery of Whitby, as it was of her disciple Bosa, who replaced Wilfrid as Bishop of York when he was exiled in 678. Others of this outlook included Cedd and Eata, who also became bishops and that 'gentle and attractive teacher' Egfrid, who lived much of his life as a monk in Leinster and who was the driving force behind the Frisian mission of Willibrord. It was Egfrid who finally won over the monks of Iona on the Easter question.

So there were Angles who clung to the 'Irish' date and refused to accept the decisions of Whitby and there were Irish and Hibernophile Angles who accepted them. There were others, most obviously Wilfrid himself, who were adamant advocates of the catholic date.

The synod of Whitby is sometimes presented as the occasion on which 'Roman' uniformity was imposed throughout Britain, with the elimination of local Celtic traditions. In fact the synod dealt with two issues: the date of Easter and the question of the way a monk's hair should be cut. The Irish had other distinctive customs, many shared with the British, with which they continued after this synod. The most significant concerned baptism, in which the Roman practice required confirmation by a bishop, whereas the Irish rite allowed chrismation by the priest. In this the Irish were at one with the Eastern churches and with modern Orthodox practice, and they came into line with Rome only in the thirteenth century. Over time, local variations in practice would tend to disappear, but there is no reason to believe that Whitby required the elimination of all Irish traditions.

To judge from Eddius, some of Wilfrid's followers regarded the Northern Irish and British as schismatics or heretics. It is possible that Wilfrid himself did so. If so, he is in the company of Cuthbert, that most Irish of the English saints. In his final address to his brethren as he lay dying, Cuthbert warned them to have no dealings with those who 'have wandered from the Catholic faith, either through not celebrating Easter at the proper time or through evil living'. Contrasts are often drawn between Cuthbert and Wilfrid. Cuthbert is portrayed as a gentle hermit in the Irish tradition, in contrast to the autocratic Wilfrid of the Roman tradition. On the one important issue that divided Irish practice from the Roman – the date of Easter – they were at one. These deathbed instructions of Cuthbert show an intolerance of divergence on this matter that is more extreme than anything we know of Wilfrid.

Epilogue

Wilfrid the Saint

Brought up in obedience to his parents, to the disabled Cudda and to Queen Eanfled, Wilfrid naturally followed the instruction and direction of Archdeacon Boniface in Rome and of his 'father' Annemund in Lyon. Having the Word of God by heart, his speech was rich in biblical reference and all his actions were seen in the light of the commandments of Christ. Thoroughly grounded in ecclesiastical order and law in the two great centres of Lyon and Rome, Wilfrid was aware of the continuous 'apostolic' tradition of the living Church and of the importance of maintaining it in its fulness.

His own authority came above all from his love of the gospel and his obedience to the word of God. The loyalty and love that he inspired in others – those crowds of his monks, for example, who came to greet him on his return from Rome in his old age – was based on the fact that they saw him as a rock, a man of ever-stable and unshakeable faith, to be relied upon, even in the most adverse circumstances. He could sing the psalms with joy when thrown into solitary confinement in a dark cell. He could run to meet a martyr's death as a young man in Lyon; fearless in the face of death, because he was confident in the risen Christ.

Wilfrid's work as abbot, bishop and missionary all flowed from this unshakeable faith. He was able to open a window into heaven. This inspired the trust that led to the great endowments of church and monastery that remained as external witness to the presence of the Holy Spirit in his life.

The devout pilgrim who gathered holy relics of the saints for the inspiration and healing of his newly converted people was himself sanctified. After his death, the Abbess of Oundle, Cynithrid, washed the cloak on which Wilfrid's body had been laid out. A poor nun with a withered arm saw the cloak in the soapy water and, lifting up her lifeless hand with the good one, plunged it into the water and rubbed it with the cloak. The fingers straightened out and her hand came back to life. Like the woman with the issue of blood who was cured by touching the hem of Christ's garment, she 'gave thanks to God, praising him for his wonderful works'.

Outside the monastery at Oundle, a tent was erected. One of the abbots laid out his robe and on this the dead Wilfrid was laid. His body was washed and vested. Wrapping the remains in linen, the monks placed them on a carriage and accompanied them all the way to Ripon, chanting as they went.

His people at Ripon came out to meet the cortège, hardly any of them able to fight back their tears. When the moment came for the departed Wilfrid to be taken into his own great basilica of St Peter, they managed to find their voices and sing the canticles and hymns appointed for the reception of the body. There in Ripon, in his fortieth year as bishop and the seventy-sixth year of his life, St Wilfrid was buried.

He was succeeded by his nominee, Acca, who commemorated him daily in the celebration of the Eucharist and had every Thursday, the day of his death, celebrated as a festival. On each anniversary of Wilfrid's death, the new abbot gave away one tenth of all his herds and flocks to the poor.

On the first anniversary of his death, all the abbots and bishops from north, south, east and west gathered with the local people to celebrate the feast. At the end of the celebrations, which had begun with the vigil the evening before, they went out to sing compline in the twilight. 'Suddenly a wonderful white arc shone out before them in the heavens, encircling the entire monastery.' The heavens bore witness to the light brought to many peoples by the first English apostle.

Notes

1   W. Goffart, *The Narrators of Barbarian History 550–800*. Princeton University Press, NJ, 1988. The chapter entitled 'Bede and the ghost of Bishop Wilfrid' is the most interesting discussion of the issues.
2   G. F. Browne, *Theodore and Wilfrith*. SPCK, London, 1897.
3   D. H. Farmer, 'Saint Wilfrid' in D. P. Kirby (ed.), *Saint Wilfrid at Hexham*. Oriel, 1974

Acknowledgements and Suggested Reading

✦✦

This short life of St Wilfrid is based on the account completed soon after his death by Eddius Stephanus, together with the sections in Bede's *Ecclesiastical History* that refer to Wilfrid. All direct quotations in the text, unless otherwise attributed, are taken from the Penguin translations of these two works. They are:

Eddius Stephanus, *Life of Wilfrid* in *The Age of Bede*, translated by J. F. Webb, Penguin Books, 1965.

Bede, *A History of the English Church and People*, translated by Leo Sherley-Price, Penguin Books, 1955. See especially Book V Chapter 19, pages 305–13.

The Age of Bede also contains Bede's *Life of Cuthbert* and his *Lives of the Abbots of Wearmouth and Jarrow*.

Bede's *Letter to Egbert* provides an invaluable insight into the state of the church in Northumbria in the early eighth century. This is available in the Oxford World Classics edition of Bede's *Ecclesiastical History*, translated by Judith McClure and Roger Collins (Oxford University Press, 1994).

I would like to thank Professor Gerald Bonner for lending me his copy of William Trent Foley's doctoral thesis *St Wilfrid of York as Pius Pater* (Chicago, Illinois, 1984) and to Winifred Lees for her careful reading of the text and her helpful suggestions.

Index and Glossary

119